COOKING IN WEST AFRICA

A Colonial Guide

Muriel R. Tew (Lady Tew)

Published by Jeppestown Press,
10A Scawfell St, London, E2 8NG, United Kingdom.

First published as *Cooking in West Africa Made Easier*,
by M. R. Tew, 1920.

Reproduced by kind permission of the copyright holder,
David Tew.

Introduction © Copyright David Saffery 2007
Lady (Muriel R.) Tew © Copyright David Tew 2007
Cover design © Copyright Chris Eason 2007

Illustrations are taken from *The Nigeria Handbook* (London, 1936: West Africa Publicity Ltd.) and *Cooking in West Africa Made Easier*.

Front cover shows (clockwise from top left) *Harmattan*, Abuja, Nigeria (http://www.flickr.com/photos/kippster/); *'African Eggplant'* at Kedougou, Senegal (http://www.flickr.com/photos/gbaku/); District Officer, Obuasi, Ghana 1915; *Peppas!*, Abeokuta, Nigeria (http://www.flickr.com/photos/i_level_news/). Back cover shows (clockwise from top left) map of Lagos c1935; Muriel Tew; Muriel Tew; DC's bungalow, Kibbi, Ghana 1915 (images of Muriel Tew © David Tew 2007).

ISBN: 0-9553936-7-1
ISBN 13:   978-0-9553936-7-9

All Rights Reserved. No part of this publication may be reproduced, stored in a retrieval system, or transmitted, in any form or by any means, electronic, mechanical, photocopying, recording, scanning or otherwise, except as described below, without the permission in writing of the Publisher. Copying is not permitted except for personal use, to the extent permitted by national copyright law. Requests for permission for other kinds of copying, such as copying for general distribution, for advertising or promotional purposes, for creating new collective works, or for resale, and other enquiries, should be addressed to the Publisher.

COOKING
---IN---
WEST AFRICA
---MADE---
EASIER
By M. R. TEW

*"Fate cannot harm me,
I have dined to-day."*

LIVERPOOL:
C. Tinling & Co., Ltd., Printers, 53, Victoria Street
1920

2007 Introduction

Muriel Tew was born in England in 1881; one of the nine children of Robert Watts Davies, a retired Royal Navy captain originally from Prince Edward Island in Canada, and Frances Ramsbotham, from Sussex.

In 1911 she married Mervyn Tew, a clergyman's son from Hampshire who had served in the Anglo-Boer War before joining the civil service in Nigeria in 1904. By 1911 Mervyn Tew had risen to the rank of Crown Solicitor, and became a barrister at Lincoln's Inn two years later before returning to Nigeria as a legal adviser. Unusually, Muriel Tew joined him there. Unusually, because government advice suggested that the hot, humid conditions of West Africa were particularly hazardous for women and children—in fact, preference for administrative appointments in the region was given to unmarried men, and until after the Second World War few wives applied for the official permission required to join their husbands in Nigeria, Sierra Leone, the Gold Coast, Cameroons and Gambia.

Because there were so few British women in West Africa, almost all cooking was carried out by native cooks, most of whom appear to have been extremely competent at reproducing their employers' favourite British recipes. Kitchens were usually located in the servants' compound well away from the main house, and most colonists employed a substantial number of domestic staff. In Kintampo in the Gold Coast (now Ghana) in 1916, for example, Laura Boyle engaged for herself and her husband a cook, cook's mate, valet/houseboy, housemaid and a dozen more men "who are hammock or garden boys as circumstances dictate".

Part of the historical interest of this work lies in the way it demonstrates a key difference between the cuisines of British settler colonies of East and South Africa, and the West African colonies where permanent white settlement—except for small numbers of civil servants and traders—was practically unknown.

Cookery books of the same vintage from southern and East Africa contain dishes using a wide range of local and indigenous fruits, vegetables, grains and meats. In these regions recipes for preparing giraffe sausages and roast monitor lizard are found alongside dishes such as the East African staple *irio*: a tasty mixture of starch and fresh maize kernels, seasoned with a relish of pumpkin leaves.

In contrast, the flavour of Muriel Tew's book is undeniably British. While many of her recipes are adapted for the challenges of catering in a climate utterly different from that of her native country, and with raw materials that in many instances were unfamiliar, or inadequate for the effort of reproducing British cuisine in West Africa, it is notable that only one or two recipes offer what might be described as a genuinely West African flavour (I am thinking here particularly of her recipes for Ground Nut Soup (closely related to the Brazilian ground-nut *vatapa* sauce, itself brought from West and Central Africa by slaves) and Lentil Cakes (similar deep-fried patties are known as *akras* in Jamaica and *akara* in Ghana and Nigeria)).

This difference between the two cuisines reflects the colonial experience in various regions of British Africa: in East and southern Africa large numbers of white settlers lived off the land, growing their own food and often adopting some of the foodstuffs, ingredients and agricultural products of the indigenous people they displaced. In West Africa, on the other hand, colonial administrators relied on local farmers and European imported foodstuffs to supply ingredients for household cookery; agricultural expertise was applied to the improvement of cash crops for export (cocoa, palm oil and rubber) rather than producing food for local settlers.

Mervyn Tew became a judge in 1923 and in 1929 was installed as Chief Justice of Sierra Leone; he left the colonial judicial service three years later, and was knighted shortly before retiring from the service. (Sir Mervyn became so bored in retirement that he returned to the Gold Coast to work as a solicitor for a friend.) Lady Tew came out to Kumasi in 1936, and caught sleeping sickness; after recovering she returned to England, where she died in 1941.

Muriel Tew's recipes are clear, concise and well-written. Part of the charm and interest of this book lies in the matter-of-fact way the author offers instructions for compromise: if you have no English yeast, by all means use native yeast to bake bread; if you happen not to possess a large saucepan to boil hams, employ a clean kerosene tin; if your cook is not good at making pastry cases, use bread instead (as in the recipe for Dresden Patties). The impression overall is of a calm and practical housekeeper.

This book offers an unique view of the development of European cuisine in West Africa during the colonial period, and helps to illuminate the social history of the region. Almost ninety years after its publication, it stands testament to the courage and resourcefulness of women like Muriel Tew. Enjoy this book and its recipes.

Lady (Muriel R.) Tew

My mother was born in 1881. She had a year at Cheltenham Ladies' College under the famous Miss Beale. She met her husband Mervyn Tew when he was a schoolmaster, but he joined the Colonial Service in 1904 as a District Officer. In 1910 he was invalided home after being struck on the head while asleep by a disaffected local.

He transferred to the legal side in 1911, when they married. They went out to Nigeria and remained in Nigeria and the Cameroons during the 1914-18 War. Her husband was forbidden to enlist in the Army in 1914 by the Colonial Office. He must have explained to her the difficulties in catering faced by young district officers, often on their own.

When things began to return to normal in 1919 she had the idea of preparing a cookery book to help such young officers. So she prepared her book on practical lines. She returned to England in 1920 to have a baby, and took the opportunity to get 500 copies of her book printed in Liverpool and marketed by Messrs. MacSymon's, Shipping Agents, with the advice of their manager, Mr. Nuttall. It was well reviewed and sold out. Her husband was surprised to be greeted with "So you're the husband of Mrs. Tew's Cookery Book."

In 1923 they were in Northern Nigeria, where her ability as a horsewoman impressed the locals, not used to European ladies riding. Her friends in the Service nicknamed her 'Tod Sloan', after the famous jockey! She remained in West Africa on and off till 1936, when she was bitten by a tsetse fly and contracted sleeping sickness. Surprisingly she survived, but never returned to the Coast and died of cancer in 1941.

David Tew, 2007

Contents

2007 INTRODUCTION	V
LADY (MURIEL R.) TEW	IX
CONTENTS	XI
PREFACE.	17
SOUPS	21
TO MAKE STOCK FOR SOUPS.	21
CHICKEN STOCK.	21
CHICKEN BROTH.	22
GROUND NUT SOUP.	23
LENTIL SOUP	24
MACARONI SOUP	26
RICE SOUP	26
TOMATO SOUP	27
FISH	31
BOILED FISH	31
BAKED FISH.	31
FISH CAKES	32
FISH CROQUETTES.	33
FISH FRIED IN BATTER	33
FRICASSEE OF FISH.	35
KEDGEREE	36
FISH OMELETTE.	36
FISH PIE WITH POTATO CRUST	37
FISH PUDDING	38
FISH SALAD	38
A SIMPLE SALAD DRESSING.	39
SCALLOPED FISH.	41
FISH STEAK—BAKED.	41
FISH STEAK—FRIED.	42
STEAMED FISH.	42
ENTREES	45
BEEF OLIVES.	45
CHICKEN CUTLETS.	46
CURRIED EGGS.	46
AN EASY CURRY.	47
DRESDEN PATTIES.	48
MUTTON CUTLETS.	49
MUTTON HOT-POT.	51

RICE CUTLETS.	51
SPAGHETTI AND GRAVY.	52
STEWED KIDNEYS.	53
STUFFED ONIONS.	53
STUFFED TOMATOES.	54
TIMBALE OF CHICKEN.	55

VEGETABLES   57

HINTS ON COOKING VEGETABLES.	57
FRENCH BEANS.	57
HARICOT BEANS.	57
TO BOIL CABBAGE.	58
CARROTS.	58
LENTIL CAKES.	58
MASHED POTATOES.	59
STEWED ONIONS WITH WHITE SAUCE.	60
PAW-PAW.	60
TO BOIL POTATOES.	60
NEW POTATOES.	61
POTATO CAKES.	61
POTATO CHIPS.	62
POTATO CHIPS.	63
POTATOES A LA MAITRE D'HOTEL.	63
POTATO RIBBONS.	63
SAUTE POTATOES.	64
SPINACH.	64
SPINACH EGGS.	65
TURNIPS.	65

MEAT.   67

RULES FOR ROASTING BEEF OR MUTTON.	67
TO MAKE THE GRAVY.	67
STEWING.	67
TO BROIL CHOPS AND STEAKS.	68
TO BOIL A HAM.	68
BEEF ROLL.	68
GATEAU OF COLD MEAT.	71
PRESSED HUMP.	71
STEWED HUMP.	72
LIVER AND BACON.	72
MEAT PASTIES.	73
MEAT PIE.	75
POTATO PIE.	78
A GOOD STEW.	79
TOAD-IN-THE-HOLE.	81

PUDDINGS, PASTRY AND SWEETS   83

HINTS ON MAKING PUDDINGS.	83
USEFUL HINTS ABOUT PASTRY.	83
BATTER PUDDING.	84
BREAD AND JAM FRITTERS.	84
CALIFORNIA PUDDING.	85
CARAMEL PUDDING.	85
CHOCOLATE JELLY.	86
CHOCOLATE SOUFFLE.	88
CORNFLOUR MOULD.	88
COCOA MOULD.	89
CUSTARD—TO SERVE WITH FRUIT.	89
CUSTARD—BAKED.	89
BAKED DUFF.	90
STEAMED DUFF.	91
STEAMED DUFF.	92
DAINTY PUDDING.	92
EGG JELLIES.	93
FRITTERS.	93
FRUIT TART.	94
GOLDEN TOAST.	95
BAKED JAM ROLL.	96
LEMON SPONGE.	96
MANGO FOOL.	97
MANGO FOOL.	98
MARMALADE PUDDING.	98
MOCK COFFEE MOULD.	99
OPEN JAM OR TREACLE TART.	99
PANCAKES.	100
PINEAPPLE SWEET.	101
PRINCESS PUDDING OR SOUFFLE.	101
PLAIN SWEET PASTRY FINGERS.	102
QUEEN OF PUDDINGS.	103
QUEEN OF PUDDINGS.	104
RICE MERINGUE.	105
SAUCER OR WAFER PUDDING.	105
STONE CREAM.	106
SWEET OMELETTE.	106
SUMMER PUDDING.	107
TARTLETS.	107
JAM TURNOVERS.	108
SUET PUDDING—BOILED.	108
SUET PUDDING—BAKED.	110
A SIMPLE TRIFLE.	111
WEST RIDING PUDDING.	111
SAVOURIES.	**113**
ANCHOVY TOAST.	113

CAULIFLOWER AU GRATIN.	113
CURRIED EGGS ON TOAST.	114
CHEESE OMELETTE.	114
CHEESE SAVOURY FOR TOAST.	115
CHEESE STRAWS.	115
CHEESE PUDDING.	116
DEVILLED FOWL'S LEGS.	117
BAKED EGGS.	117
BUTTERED OR SCRAMBLED EGGS.	118
BUTTERED OR SCRAMBLED EGGS.	119
EGG FRITTERS.	119
POACHED EGGS.	120
SAVOURY EGGS.	120
KIDNEY OMELETTE.	121
MACARONI CHEESE.	121
SAVOURY OMELETTE.	122
SAVOURY ONIONS.	123
SAVOURY RICE—I.	123
SAVOURY RICE—II.	124
TOMATO OMELETTE.	124
TOMATO TOAST.	125
SAVOURY TOMATOES.	125
WELSH RARE-BIT.	127

BREAD, CAKES ETC. — 129

USEFUL HINTS FOR CAKE MAKING.	129
BREAD.	129
BREAKFAST ROLLS.	130
CURRANT CAKE.	131
CHOCOLATE CAKE.	132
CHOCOLATE CAKES.	132
GINGER CAKE.	133
GINGER SLAB.	134
MILK CAKES.	134
ROCK BUNS.	135
CURRANT CAKE.	135
SANDWICH CAKE.	136
BUTTER CREAM.	136
SCONES	137
SPONGE CAKE	137
'SQUASHED FLY' BISCUITS.	140
WAFER BISCUITS.	140
WATER BISCUITS.	141

SAUCES. — 143

GENERAL RULES FOR MAKING SAUCES.	143
BROWN SAUCE.	143

BROWN GLAZE FOR BEEF ROLL	143
MAYONNAISE SAUCE FOR SALADS—1.	144
MAYONNAISE SAUCE—2.	144
ONION SAUCE.	145
WHITE SAUCE.	145
SWEET SAUCE.	146
PARSLEY SAUCE.	146
CAPER SAUCE.	146
CHEESE SAUCE.	146
FISH SAUCE.	146

SICK ROOM 147

THIN BARLEY WATER.	147
THICK BARLEY WATER.	147
BARLEY MILK.	147
BARLEY WATER MADE WITH PATENT BARLEY.	148
BEEF TEA.	148
CUP OF ARROWROOT.	148
GRUEL WITH PATENT GROATS.	149
LEMONADE.	149
SAVOURY CUSTARD.	150
OXO.	150

ODDS AND ENDS. 151

SERVICEABLE MEASURES.	151
TO TAKE STAINS OFF CUPS AND TEAPOTS.	151
TO CLEAN GREASY PLATES OR KNIVES, ETC.	152
IRONMOULDS.	152
LUX.	152
TO REMOVE INK STAINS FROM LINEN.	152
TO ABSORB DAMP IN A CUPBOARD.	153
LAMP CLEANING.	153
SOAP.	153
HOMEMADE DRIPPING.	153
TO CLARIFY FAT.	154
FAT FOR FRYING.	154
TO MAKE BROWNING FOR GRAVIES AND SOUPS.	154
TO SKIN TOMATOES.	155
PICKLE FOR MEAT—1.	155
PICKLE FOR MEAT—2.	155
SALT BEEF.	156
HOME-MADE BAKING POWDER.	156
ORANGE MARMALADE.	156
PAW-PAW JAM.	157
HOME-MADE TOFFEE—1	157
HOME-MADE TOFFEE—2.	158
PEPPERMINT CREAMS.	158

LEMON CURD.	159
TO BLANCH ALMONDS.	159
OATMEAL PORRIDGE.	159
HINTS FOR THE COOK'S BOX	**161**
A FEW SUBSTITUTES.	163
BIBLIOGRAPHY	**164**
ACKNOWLEDGEMENTS	**165**

PREFACE.

The apparent desire on the part of many friends in Nigeria for a Cookery Book containing easy recipes has encouraged me to try to compile one. Cooking in this country will never be easy, but I have tried to choose dishes which a native cook should be able to turn out well with little difficulty.

Some of the recipes appear to be formidable and long— but I have given them in detail—and the making of them is not as difficult as it might appear.

"Hope springs eternal in the 'housewife's' breast" at the sight of a new Cookery Book—the hope that the difficult problem of catering will be solved at last. This book will bring disappointment as others have done, but if the recipes enable the cook to give his Master a variety of plain dishes and frequent change, if only in the matter of serving the "dish," it will not have been written in vain.

M. R. T.

The quantities mentioned in these recipes are sufficient for two persons.

COOKING IN WEST AFRICA

A Colonial Guide

SOUPS

TO MAKE STOCK FOR SOUPS.

About fourpenny worth of bones and meat from the market.
1 onion.
A little salt and pepper.
2 breakfastcups of water.
A native cooking pot with a lid.

Take the fat off the bones, wipe them with a cloth, chop them in two if too big for the pot; put them with the scraps of meat into the pot; cover them with water and add the salt. Bring them to the boil; if any scum or dirt rises to the top, take it off with a spoon and throw it away. Now clean the onion, cut it into four pieces and add it to the stock. Pull the pot away from the fire; let it stay on the side of the stove and simmer, or cook gently for two or three hours. Tilt the lid of the pot so that the steam can get away. Then strain it into a basin, and when it is cold take the fat off the top very carefully with a spoon.

Don'ts—Don't forget this is not soup. Don't forget to make this when you come back from the market with the bones—you make it up into soup later on. Don't forget that soups should never look greasy, so you must make the stock early—let it get cold and then take the fat off the top.

CHICKEN STOCK.

Remarks—If you are having chicken for a meal, tell the cook to keep the "trimmings"; they make a good stock for soups. The "trimmings" consist of liver, gizzard, neck, bones.

2 breakfastcups of water.
1 onion.
1 clove stuck in the onion.

½ teaspoon of salt.
A little pepper.
(3 small carrots, 2 turnips and a little parsley if possible.)

Put the trimmings from the chicken into a native pot or saucepan. Add the onion and clove and salt. Pour over them the 2 cups of water. Bring slowly to the boil. Look inside the pot every now and then, and take off the scum that rises to the top with a spoon; throw the scum away. Now put the other vegetables in if you have any. Boil up again, and then draw the pot to one side of the stove and let it simmer for quite an hour. By this time there should only be about the quantity of stock. Put the sieve over a basin and strain the stock into it. Let it stand till you want it to make into soup.

CHICKEN BROTH.

1 fowl.
3 breakfastcups of cold water.
1 onion with a clove stuck in it.
1 teaspoon of salt.
Some pepper.
A little nutmeg.

Clean the fowl, cut off its wings and legs, break up the body, and put all into a native pot or a saucepan. Wash and scrape the feet and put them also into the pot with the salt and pepper. Add the 3 cups of water, and put on the fire to boil. When the scum rises to the top of the water, take it off with a spoon and throw it away. Do not have a very fierce fire. The broth should not begin to boil for about 20 minutes or an hour. As soon as the water jumps throw in the onion and clove and the nutmeg. (If you have any carrots and turnips, wash them and cut them up, and add them now.) Throwing in the vegetables will stop the water boiling; so make it boil again, and have the lid half off so that the steam can get away. Now put the pot on one side of the stove so that the soup does not boil any more it must just simmer gently for quite an hour to draw all the goodness out of the meat and bones. Then put the sieve over a large basin, pour the soup through it, and let it get cold. About of an hour before you want to serve it, take off any fat there may be on the top of the soup. Put it into a saucepan, and heat it. Small squares of toasted bread are good served with this soup.

Don'ts—Don't throw away the meat off the breast, legs, etc—

(a) Pick out the best pieces with a fork, cut them into little squares, and put them in the soup plates, then pour on the soup.

(b) Or they can be kept back, minced or chopped small, and used to stuff onions or tomatoes; or small rissoles made with them.

GROUND NUT SOUP.

2 breakfastcups of stock.
1 teacup of ground nuts.
teaspoon of salt.
A little pepper.

Any good stock may be used, but see that it is free from grease. Have it made some time before you want the ground nut soup; let it get cold in a basin; then remove any fat that is at the top. Roast and peel the ground nuts, then pound them quite small—to a paste (in a native mortar). Put the paste in a basin and mix with a teacup of cold water. Make the stock hot, then add the ground nut paste, and boil for ten minutes. Add the salt and pepper. Then set on one side, and heat up again inst before serving. Little squares of toast or fried bread are nice served with this soup.

To thicken this soup or any other soup—If you like the soup rather thicker, it can be done in the following way:

1 large teaspoon of cornflour or flour.
2 tablespoons of milk or water.

About ¼ of an hour before you have to serve the soup put the cornflour or flour into the basin, mix it to a cream with the milk or water (or half milk and half water). Then pour a little of the hot soup on to the thickening, and stir well. Then pour all this into the saucepan containing the remainder of the soup. If you pour the thickening straight into the hot soup it is likely to go lumpy; always pour a little of the hot liquid first on to the thickening.

Don't—Don't boil the ground nuts more than 10 minutes; longer boiling will bring the oil out of them to the top.

To make the Stock into different kinds of Soups:

LENTIL SOUP

1 breakfastcup of stock.
½ breakfastcup of red lentils.
1 onion.
1 tablespoon of dripping.
Some salt and pepper.

Soak the lentils all night in a pudding basin, cover them well with water, and drain them well next day. If the soup is wanted for dinner, begin to make it about 5 o'clock. Put the dripping in the saucepan, slice the onion, put in the lentils; put the saucepan on the fire, and stir for five minutes. Now add the cup of water, and let the soup boil gently till the lentils are quite soft. If you have a hair sieve put it over a large basin, pass the lentils through it, mashing them with the back of a wooden spoon, and scraping them off the under side of the sieve. Now put all that is in the basin back into the saucepan; add the cupful of stock, and the pepper and salt, and warm it again over the fire. Fried bread is good served with this soup. Cut a slice of bread into strips, then cut the strips into little squares, and fry them in hot fat till they are brown

Jacob & Co.'s
BISCUITS

are known the world over for their *excellent flavour and keeping qualities*...

℃ Always specify the **"JACOB" BRAND** when ordering supplies.

ESTABLISHED 1851

W. & R. JACOB & CO.
——— LIMITED ———

Biscuit Manufacturers

Dublin, London, Liverpool and **Manchester**

and crisp. Put them on a warm plate, and hand them round with the soup.

Don'ts—Don't let the lentils burn, keep enough water in the pot, and stir them every now and then.

MACARONI SOUP

A teacup of macaroni.
A breakfastcup of stock.
2 onions.
2 cloves.
Some salt and pepper.
(A few carrots and turnips if you have any.)

Begin to make this soup about 2 hours before you want it. Put the cupful of stock into a saucepan. Wash the onions, and stick a clove into each of them; and if you have other vegetables, wash, peel and scrape them, and add them to the stock. Let the soup boil gently on the side of the stove for about 2 hours. Break the macaroni into pieces about half the size of a match, throw it into a saucepan of boiling water, add a little salt and pepper. The macaroni will take about an hour to boil. When it is time to serve the soup, put a little macaroni at the bottom of each soup plate, and strain the soup over it.

Don'ts—Don't serve the vegetables with this soup—they are only put in to flavour it.

RICE SOUP

½ teacup of rice.
½ tablespoon of butter or margarine or dripping.
1½ cup of milk (teacup).
1 cups of water (breakfast cup).
1 small onion.
(1 carrot, if you have one.)
Some salt and pepper.

This soup only takes about ¼ of an hour or an hour to make. Put the butter in a saucepan and let it melt. Slice the onion (and carrot) and put them in the butter, let the juices come out of them, but do not let them fry brown. Now put 1 cups of water in the saucepan with the onion, etc. Wash the rice and add it to the saucepan, and let all boil till the rice is soft. Add salt and pepper. Then put the hair sieve over a basin, and strain the rice and vegetables through, mashing them with the back of a spoon. Put the soup back into the saucepan, add the cup of milk, and let it boil—then serve. This is a nourishing soup.

Don'ts—Don't boil native rice as long as the "English" rice. It takes about half the time. Twenty minutes for "English" rice; 10 minutes for native rice.

TOMATO SOUP

4 large or 8 small tomatoes.
1 or 2 onions.
2 breakfastcups of water.
1 teaspoon salt.
1 small teaspoon castor sugar.
A little pepper.
A teacup of milk and water mixed.

Wash the tomatoes and onion, and cut them all into four pieces. Put them in a clean saucepan, and sprinkle them with the salt, pepper and sugar. Pour the 2 cups of water over them, and put them on the fire to boil. When it begins to bubble and jump put the saucepan on one side, and let it cook slowly for nearly 2 hours till the soup looks thick (like a purée). About of an hour before you serve it, put a sieve over a basin, pass the soup through it into the basin, mashing it, and helping it through with the back of a wooden spoon. Pour the teacup of milk and water into a clean saucepan and let it boil, then add it to the soup in the basin; pour all back into the saucepan to keep hot till it is time to serve it. Fried bread squares are good with this soup.

Don'ts—Don't pour the cold milk and water (Ideal milk diluted) into the soup or it may curdle—it must boil first and then be added. Don't let this soup be too thin.

BANK of BRITISH WEST AFRICA, LTD.

... *Established* 1894 ...

Bankers to the Governments of the Colonies of the Gambia, Sierra Leone, Gold Coast and Nigeria.

HEAD OFFICE: 17 & 18, LEADENHALL ST., LONDON, E.C.3.
Liverpool Office: **WEST AFRICA HOUSE, 25, WATER STREET.**
Manchester Office: **106 & 108, PORTLAND STREET.**
Bradford Office: **17, IVEGATE.**
New York Office: **100, BEAVER STREET.**

Authorised and Subscribed Capital - £2,000,000
Called-up Capital - - - - - - £800,000
Reserve - - - - - - - - £378,750

Directors:

The Rt. Hon. The Earl of Selborne, K.G., G.C.M.G. (Chairman).
Clifford B. Edgar, Esq., M.P.   D. Q. Henriques, Esq., J.P.
Geo. Miller, Esq.   W. F. Moore, Esq.   Geo. W. Neville, Esq.
J. W. Beaumont Pease, Esq., J.P.   Sir Owen Philipps, G.C.M.G., M.P.
Sir H. Babington Smith, K.C.B., C.S.I.
Mazzini Stuart, Esq., J.P.   O. Harrison Williams, Esq.

General Manager: Leslie Couper, C.M.G.

WEST AFRICA: *Branches:*

GAMBIA—Bathurst.   SIERRA LEONE—Freetown, Sherbro.
LIBERIA—Monrovia.   TOGOLAND—Lome.   GOLD COAST and
ASHANTI—Accra, Axim, Bekwai, Cape Coast, Coomassie, Dunkwa, Koforidua, Nsawam, Saltpond, Seccondee, Tarquah, Winnebah.
NIGERIA—Abeokuta, Calabar, Ebute Metta, Forcados, Ibadan, Jos, Kaduna, Kano, Lagos, Lokoja, Onitsha, Port Harcourt, Warri, Zaria.
CAMEROONS—Duala.   FERNANDO PO—Santa Isabel.

MOROCCO:

Casablanca, Fez, Marrakesh, Mazagan, Rabat, Saffi, Tangier.
CANARY ISLANDS—Las Palmas.   EGYPT—Alexandria.

AGENCIES THROUGHOUT MOROCCO, WEST AFRICA, EGYPT.

FISH

BOILED FISH

Put some water in a large saucepan or fish kettle. Put it on the fire to get hot. Wash the fish well in cold water, and put it on an old dish or a strainer. When the water in the saucepan is warm put the dish or strainer with the fish on it into the pan, and add a little salt. There must be enough water to cover the fish. Let it simmer—that is, the water must not jump about and boil hard, but it must be near the fire and moving quietly. Look inside the pot now and then, and if there is any dirt on the top of the water take it off with a spoon and throw it away. When the skin begins to crack then the fish has boiled long enough. About 20 minutes for a medium-sized piece of fish. Take it out very carefully, dish and all if possible, put it on a hot plate, and serve with a white sauce. The sauce can be served separately, and the fish and dish decorated with slices of lime.

Don'ts—Don't forget to put an old plate or dish, or strainer under the fish before putting it into the pot—it will stick to the pot if you don't, and be difficult to get out.

BAKED FISH.

Remarks—This is a good way to cook a chumpy piece of fish, and is very easy—and all the flavour is kept in the fish.

A thick piece of fish—a middle cut.
A baking dish.
A little butter.
A little pepper.
A little salt.
A sheet of clean paper.

Rub the baking dish over with butter or oil. Wash the fish, dry it with a cloth, and put it on the tin. Sprinkle a little salt and pepper over it. Spread some butter on to the clean piece of paper, and cover the fish closely with it. Put this in the oven, and when the fish is cooked take off the paper. It will take about 10 or 20 minutes to cook. Put the fish on a hot dish, and pour over the juice that is on the baking dish. Serve very hot; and decorate the top of fish and sides of the dish with cut lime. If you have some parsley, chop it very fine, and sprinkle over the fish—this looks better still. Serve a white sauce with this.

FISH CAKES

A breakfastcup of cold boiled fish.
½ teacup of rice.
A teaspoon onion.
A teaspoon chopped parsley, if you have any.
2 eggs.
A little salt and pepper.
1 tablespoon milk.
2 tablespoons fine breadcrumbs.
½ tablespoon of butter.

See that you have everything you want on the table before you begin. Wash the rice, then throw it into a saucepan of boiling water, and let it boil till quite soft. Strain off the water. Pick the fish off the bones with a fork in each hand. Chop up the onion quite small (and the parsley). Put the butter in a small saucepan. Add the milk, and when they are hot put in the pieces of fish, the rice, the yellow of one egg, salt, pepper, onion (and parsley). Stir all well together. Take the saucepan off the fire, and take out one tablespoonful of the mixture. Make it into a ball, then flatten it a little to make a cake. Break the other egg on to a plate, mix it well with a knife. Put the cake on to the egg plate, and brush it over with a clean feather dipped in the egg. Sprinkle fine breadcrumbs all over it. Make up the other cakes in the same way, and fry them in hot fat.

Don'ts—Don't forget to have clean hands before you begin. Don't leave any bones in the fish. Don't let the mixture be too dry and stodgy. Don't try and fry till the fat is hot—a blue smoke should be rising out of the pan—then it is ready.

FISH CROQUETTES.

Remarks—These are made exactly like the fish cakes, only the shape is altered. If you cannot get much variety in the way of food, it is sometimes a relief to see it served somewhat differently—served on a different dish even makes some change.

Ingredients: same as for Fish Cakes.

For croquettes take a tablespoonful of the mixture, and shape it as much as possible like a good-sized sausage. Dip it in egg, then sprinkle well with breadcrumbs. See that your fat is hot in the frying-pan, and fry. Another change is to grease a tin plate, shape the mixture as much like a fish as possible, brush it over with egg, and bake it for of an hour.
Don'ts—Don't let the mixture be too dry.

FISH FRIED IN BATTER

Some fresh fish cut away from the bones with a sharp knife. Divide it into nice-sized pieces, about the size of the bowl of a tablespoon.

FOR THE BATTER—

4 tablespoons of flour.
1 teacup of water.
1 tablespoon of salad (or nut) oil.
A little salt.

London and Kano Trading Company
Limited

KANO
SOKOTO
··· ETC. ···

LAGOS
ZARIA
··· ETC. ···

Put the flour in a basin with a pinch of salt, then stir in gradually the salad oil and the water, a little of each at a time. (Ground nut oil will do instead of salad oil.) The batter must stand a long time before you use it. Quite ½ an hour—1 hour is not too long. Take the fish, dip the pieces in the batter, taking them in and out on the point of a sharp piece of stick. Have some hot fat in the frying-pan, and fry the fish in this.

Don'ts—Don't forget that a blue smoke should rise out of the frying-pan before the fat is hot enough for frying.

FRICASSEE OF FISH.

A piece of cooked fish about the size of a breakfast cup.
A teacup of water.
½ teacup of milk.
Some nutmeg.
A little salt.
1 tablespoon of butter.
1 tablespoon of flour.
A lime—or piece of lemon.

Put the water in a saucepan. Take the fish off the bones and put them (the bones) in the water, with the nutmeg and salt. When this has boiled for an hour, strain it, and stir it into the milk. Put the butter into a saucepan, and when it has melted, stir in the flour and mix well for a minute. Pour in the milk, stir well, and let it boil till the flour is cooked—about 10 minutes. You should now have a white sauce, smooth and thick—if too thick add a little more water. Now put the pieces of fish into this sauce, and let it cook gently for of an hour. Sere it with small pieces of toast—arrange the toast round the dish with pieces of lime.

Don'ts—Don't let the milk sauce burn or be lumpy, stir it well.

KEDGEREE

A breakfastcup of cold boiled fish.
3 tablespoons rice.
2 eggs.
1 tablespoons of butter.
A little salt.
A pinch of cayenne pepper.

Wash the rice and throw it into a saucepan of boiling water, let it boil for 10 minutes (if native rice), 20 minutes (if "English" rice). Drain away the water and let the rice dry. Put the eggs carefully into boiling water, and boil them for 10 minutes. Dip them in cold water. Break the shell and peel it off. Then cut the whites into small squares. Melt the butter in a stewpan, and add the rice to it. Stir them together. Then add the fish, and white of egg. cayenne pepper, salt (and nutmeg, if you like it). Mix all well together, and turn out neatly on a hot dish. Sprinkle the yellow of the egg over it. If you have a sieve, place the yolks of the eggs on it, then press them through with the back of a spoon. They should fall out underneath all curly. Take them up carefully on the blade of a knife and shake them over the kedgeree. This mixture may be put into a basin and turned out as a mould.

FISH OMELETTE.

Remarks—A very appetising breakfast or lunch dish. Prawns are excellent for it. If they cannot be bought fresh (as in Lagos), open a tin and use half of the contents, emptying the rest into a basin. (These can be used for a savoury or for "small chop.") If the prawns are fresh, see that they are washed and shelled before putting them in the omelette.

FOR THE OMELETTE—

2 eggs.
1 tablespoon butter or nut oil.

A little salt.
4 teaspoon chopped parsley if possible.

Break the eggs into a basin and beat them together with the egg beater till they look light and fluffy. Sprinkle in the salt, pepper and parsley. Melt the butter in the small frying-pan; when it is quite hot pour in the egg mixture. Let them set just a little. Then lay the prawns on the top. As soon as the edges of the omelette look firm or set, fold it in half, helping it over with the handle of a spoon. It should now be this shape ◖ Cook lightly for a moment, then place it on a hot dish, and serve at once. If you cannot get prawns, use about a tablespoonful of some cooked fish, free from bones.

Don'ts—Don't begin to make an omelette long before it is wanted. A ¼ of an hour before serving time is soon enough. Don't forget that the longer you beat the eggs the lighter will be the omelette. Seven minutes is a good time.

FISH PIE WITH POTATO CRUST

2 breakfastcups of cold fish.
6 or 7 good-sized potatoes.
1 tablespoon of dripping.
½ teacup of milk and water (Ideal milk).
Some pepper and salt.

Boil the potatoes, then squeeze them through a masher, or put them in a basin, and break them up with a fork till there are no lumps left. Put the dripping into a small saucepan, with half the milk and water, and when the dripping has melted, stir it and the milk into the potatoes, and beat them up well with a fork. Break the fish into small pieces; grease a pie dish, put in the fish, sprinkle with pepper and salt, a teaspoonful of sauce, if you like it. Add the rest of the milk. Cover the fish with the mashed potatoes, smooth them neatly with a knife dipped in hot water, then mark it neatly with a fork, and bake it for of an hour, and the top must be nice and brown.

Don'ts—Don't leave any bones in the fish. Don't make it too dry and stodgy; add more milk and water if it does not seem enough.

FISH PUDDING

2 breakfastcups of cooked fish (about 1 lb. of fish).
2 tablespoons of suet.
2 tablespoons of breadcrumbs.
2 eggs.
1 tablespoon of milk.
A little salt.
A little pepper.
A teaspoon of chopped parsley if possible.

Wash the fish, and take away all the bones and skin. Chop the suet very fine. Put the fish and suet in a pudding basin, and pound them well with a spoon. Add the breadcrumbs, eggs (parsley), salt, pepper and milk. Pound all these well together with the back of a spoon, then put them into a pudding basin, cover them with your pudding cloth, tie it round the basin with a piece of string, then bring the four corners up to the top of the basin, and pin or tie them together (like you do for a suet pudding). Have ready a large saucepan, not too full of boiling water, put an old saucer at the bottom as this keeps the bottom of the pudding basin from being burnt. Drop in the basin carefully, and boil for 1 hour. When it is done turn the pudding out on to a hot dish, and cover it with egg sauce, or serve the sauce separately.

Don'ts—Don't let the boiling water come up over the basin; Don't let the water boil away—look inside the pot occasionally, and add more from a kettle of boiling water if necessary.

FISH SALAD

Some cold fish (cooked).
2 lettuces (if possible).
3 tomatoes.
4 or 6 spring onions, or
a large onion.
2 eggs—hard boiled.

Put two eggs into boiling water, boil them for 10 minutes. Then take them out and dip them in cold water. Boil the fish and let it get cold, or use any fish left over from breakfast—see that it is fresh. Place it neatly at the bottom of the salad dish. Wash the lettuce leaves very carefully in three different waters. Then tear the leaves into small bits, or cut into narrow strips with a sharp knife. Wash the tomatoes and slice them. Wash the onions, and chop them fine—the tender green stalks of the spring onion may be cut fine too. Peel the hard-boiled eggs, and cut them into rings or into 4 pieces. Sprinkle the onion over the fish. Then the lettuce leaves. Then the slices of tomato and hard-boiled egg. Pour over the whole some salad dressing.

A SIMPLE SALAD DRESSING.

1 yolk of egg.
1 tablespoon of oil.
2 tablespoons of vinegar.
1 saltspoon of salt.
A little pepper.
1 teaspoon of made mustard.
3 tablespoons of milk
1 tablespoon of water

Put the yolk of the egg into a basin. Sprinkle on it the salt, pepper and mustard, and stir them. Then as slowly as ever you can, just drop by drop, put in the oil, stirring all the time. The mixture should now be thick. Now pour in the vinegar—not quickly, and stir till all is well mixed. Then add gradually the milk. Stir well, and pour over the fish salad.

Don'ts—Don't forget to mix hard, stirring one way all the time.

HUMPHREYS & CROOK LTD.
3, HAYMARKET, LONDON, S.W.1

Cables:
**HUMPOOK
LONDON**

Telephone:
**WHITEHALL
5342/3**

to

THE NIGERIA REGIMENT
THE GOLD COAST REGIMENT
THE SIERRA LEONE BATTALION
ROYAL WEST AFRICAN FRONTIER FORCE

**MILITARY
TAILORS
AND
COLONIAL
OUTFITTERS**

HUMPHREYS & CROOK LTD. respectfully offer their services to those who still believe that quality is the truest economy.

1850 — 1936

ESTABLISHED NEARLY 100 YEARS.

SCALLOPED FISH.

Remarks—You want small china cups or darioles for this.

A breakfastcup of cooked fish.
½ teacup of breadcrumbs.
2 teaspoons of butter.
A little pepper and salt.
2 tablespoons of water in which the fish was boiled.
2 or 4 little china cups.

Butter the cups. Sprinkle a layer of breadcrumbs on them. Then a layer of the fish, broken up into pieces with a fork, and the bones taken away. A little salt and pepper, and bits of butter put next on the fish. Cover all this with more breadcrumbs and a tiny bit of butter. Then pour a little fish liquor in (or a little milk) to moisten it, but it must not be too sloppy. Put the cups in the oven, and let them bake for 10 minutes. The top should be a golden colour like brass.

FISH STEAK—BAKED.

The middle cut of a good-sized fish.
A little butter.
Some pepper.
Some salt.
Some milk.
An oven tin.

Wash the fish, and cut the piece right through into two slabs or steaks—let them be about as thick as half a match. Put them in the oven tin, with a tablespoonful of milk and a tablespoonful of water mixed. Put a small piece of butter on each steak, some pepper and salt. Grease a clean piece of paper with the butter, and cover over the fish, and bake about 20 minutes. Serve a white sauce with it, but do not pour the sauce over the fish.

FISH STEAK—FRIED.

The middle cut of a good-sized fish.
1 egg.
Some fine breadcrumbs.
Some dripping or oil.
A frying-pan.

Cut the fish into slabs or steaks right through the backbone, wash it, and dry it with a clean cloth. Break the egg on to a plate, and beat it with a fork or knife till the white and yellow are mixed. Put the breadcrumbs on another plate. Put your saucepan on the fire with the fat, and let it get hot. Dip the fish steak first into the egg, and dab it all over with a clean feather dipped in the egg. Then put it on the plate of breadcrumbs, and cover it well both sides. If a blue smoke is rising from the frying- pan then the fat is hot enough. Put in the fish steaks, and fry them till they are brown. Serve a white sauce or egg sauce with them, separately.

STEAMED FISH.

Remarks—To cook food by steaming is said to be better, in most cases, than by boiling, as it preserves the flavour of the article being cooked, and retains the nourishing juices which are removed by boiling. It is thought to be a specially good way of cooking for invalids, but fish and meat steamed require a longer time than when boiled or roast.

A piece of good fish.
A fish kettle or large saucepan, with well-fitting lid.
A plate or basin.

If you use a large saucepan, half fill it with water, and when it is boiling put a plate over the top. Clean the fish, and wipe it with a clean cloth, then place it on the plate, and cover it with another plate that fits closely. As the water below boils away, add more boiling water from the kettle. It will take longer to steam than to boil. When it begins to crack, and leave the bones easily, it is cooked. Serve with parsley and anchovy, or egg sauce. If you use a fish kettle, place a basin in the kettle, and stand the fish on a plate on the basin, with enough water to come half way up the basin. The fish must be raised out of the water, and the lid of the fish kettle must fit well down.

Miller Brothers (of Liverpool) Ltd.

(PROVISION DEPARTMENT)

have pleasure in announcing that they are once again in a position to supply Provisions of the very best quality, packed for export by British Houses. Dealing with reliable firms only, goods of first-class quality are insured. Stocks are turned over regularly, and at all Coast Stores ample supplies can be obtained.

SPECIALITIES

Crosse and Blackwell's and Elizabeth Lazenby's bottled and tinned goods. Letham's, Hunter's and Redgate's bacon and hams. Huntley and Palmer's, Peek Frean's and Jacob's well-known biscuits. Melrose's, Lipton's and Mazawattee Teas. Schweppes, Ross's, Stretton and Caley's renowned Mineral Waters. All good brands of whiskies, gins, brandies and wines. Tobaccos, cigars and cigarettes, etc., etc.

ORDERS from customers in NORTHERN PROVINCES can now be accepted at LAGOS and every attention will be given to ensure quick despatch and safe transit. All risks in, and cost of, transport beyond store are purchasers.

BRANCHES in SOUTHERN PROVINCES: Lagos, Badagry, Abeokuta, Ibadan, Warri, Koko, Sapele, Siluko, Port Harcourt, Aba, Opobo, Calabar, Oron, Itu, &c.

BRANCHES in NORTHERN PROVINCES will be opened up in due course.

LAGOS, NOVEMBER, 1919.

ENTREES

BEEF OLIVES.

Remarks—These are only possible if you are fortunate enough to get a good sirloin of beef. They are cut from a piece of cooked sirloin.

As many thin slices of beef as possible.

For the stuffing—

3 tablespoons of breadcrumbs.
2 tablespoons of suet.
1 teaspoon of chopped parsley if possible.
¼ teaspoonful of dried herbs if possible.
A little grated nutmeg and lemon rind.
1 egg.
Salt and pepper.
2 breakfast cups of gravy.

Cut the fillet or sirloin of beef into slices about ½-inch thick and about the length of the middle finger. Put them on a board and beat them out with a wet rolling-pin. Chop up the trimmings of the beef, the suet, parsley and herbs. Put these into a basin and add the salt, pepper, nutmeg, lemon rind, the egg, and breadcrumbs Mix all together. This is for the stuffing. Put a little of this stuffing on each slice of beef. Roll it up and tie it round with a piece of cotton or string (one tie is enough). Put the two cupfuls of gravy into a stewpan, place the rolls in it and stew gently for hour (if the meat is uncooked); 20 minutes (if the meat has been cooked before).

To serve them take off the string and dish up on a hot plate—in the middle of the dish with mashed potatoes all round is a good way—and the gravy, which should be thick, poured all round.

CHICKEN CUTLETS.

The meat off a cold fowl.
½ breakfast cup of cooked mash potato or yam.
2 eggs.
2 teaspoons chopped onion.
A little grated nutmeg, pepper and salt.
1 tablespoon of fine bread crumbs or biscuit crumbs.

Chop or mince the meat off the cold fowl— put it in a mixing basin. Add onion, salt, pepper, nutmeg, yam or potato. Break one egg into a cup; if it is good beat it for a. minute with a fork and add it to all the other things in the basin. Mix all together. If it won't bind together, add a little stock; if it is too thin, add a little flour. Turn it out on to a board and shape the mixture like cutlets, and a small chicken bone can be poked in at one end. Beat up the other egg, dip the cutlets into the egg or brush them over with a clean feather. Sprinkle on them the bread crumbs and fry in hot fat.

In the centre of the dish arrange a heap of cooked peas, or mixed vegetables. Put the cutlets neatly round the peas, making them stand on their heads, as it were. Then if you have room put a tablespoonful of well mashed potato or yam at each side and at the top and bottom of the dish.

If you cannot make a. nice cutlet shape, roll the mixtures into sausage shapes, only fatter and smaller.

CURRIED EGGS.

Remarks—This is a very light, appetising dish for lunch.

4 eggs.
1 small tablespoon of flour.
3 teacup of stock.
1 teaspoon curry powder.
1 tablespoon of butter or dripping.

Put the eggs gently into boiling water; boil them for ten minutes till they are hard. Take the shells off them and cut them in half, or keep them whole, as you like best. Put the butter or dripping in a frying pan, fry the onion, then stir in the flour and curry powder. Add the stock, and let it cook slowly for lb minutes. If it gets too thick add a little boiling water. Arrange the eggs on a dish, pour the curry over them, and serve with boiled rice. Arrange the rice either round the dish or serve by itself.

AN EASY CURRY.

Remarks—This curry is rather mild, but can be made hotter to taste by adding more curry powder and native peppers. It does not profess to be an "Indian" curry.

The meat off a cooked chicken; or
A piece off a leg of mutton; or
A piece of fresh meat about the size of a large cup
1 tablespoon of dripping.
½ a large or 1 small onion.
1 tablespoon of flour.
½ tablespoon of curry powder.
1 teacup of rice.
Lime.

Boil the rice about half an hour before you want it. Put on a saucepan of water to boil. Wash the rice, and when the water is bubbling throw in the rice and let it jump about for 10 minutes (native rice), 20 minutes ("English" rice). Strain off the water and put the rice on a sieve to dry, in the oven or in the sun. Put a frying pan on the fire with the dripping in it. When a blue smoke rises put in the onion, sliced up, and let it get brown, but not burnt. Then sprinkle the flour over the onion and stir well. Add a little boiling water out of the kettle, mix well. If too thick (it thickens as it cooks) add a little more water. Let it boil and get thick till you have a tasty gravy. Now add the half spoon of curry powder (or more curry powder according to taste), a little salt, and mix well with the spoon, adding still more water if you think it is too thick. Then put in the meat to warm through. It is best cut into small pieces, like dice. Let all cook gently over the fire for about 10 minutes, stirring it so that it does not burn. Serve the rice on one dish, the curry on another, the limes cut in slices and arranged round the curry dish.

Peppers on separate saucers placed on the table.

Don'ts—Don't forget to clean the frying pan well after making the curry. If you do not, the next thing you fry in it will probably look green.

DRESDEN PATTIES.

Remarks—If your cook is not a good pastry maker, these "cases" of bread are easy to make, and quite attractive.

Slices of stale bread.
A teacup of minced meat.
2 teaspoons of chopped parsley (if possible).
1 teaspoon of chopped onion.
1 egg.
A little sauce or gravy, about 1 teaspoonful.
½ teacup of breadcrumbs.
Salt and pepper.

Cut three thick slices of bread, about 2 inches thick. Stamp out as many rounds as you can with the pastry cutter, the size of a patty or tartlet. Take out the middle very carefully from each round so as to form a case in which to put mince. Then cut a much smaller round which is to form a lid, one lid for each case. Dip the cases for a second in milk, then drain them. Chop the meat or mince it (and the parsley) and onion, put them in a saucepan on the fire, sprinkle on salt and pepper, and add enough gravy or sauce to make them moist. Break an egg, beat it with a knife, then brush each case of bread over with the egg and coat it with breadcrumbs. Have ready a pan of fat—there should be enough fat to well cover them, if possible. When a bluish smoke rises, put in the cases, two at a time, and fry them a golden brown. Drain them quickly on paper.

Have the meat mixture very hot, heap it into the cases. Place a neat lid of fried bread on the top of each. Arrange them neatly on a lace paper, and serve.

Don'ts—Don't fry the bread too hard and crisp.

MUTTON CUTLETS.

Remarks—Choose small mutton and quite the best end of the neck to make neat cutlets.

Saw off enough of the rib bones to leave the cutlets about as long as the middle finger. Cut the cutlets close against the bones with a sharp knife, making them about inch thick. Cut away a little (about 1 inch) of the meat from the ends of the bones, and scrape them quite clean. Cut away the fat, all but a thin layer. Break an egg on to a plate, mix it with a knife, dip each cutlet in the egg, then in fine breadcrumbs. Fry in fat from which a bluish smoke is rising for 3 or 4 minutes. Drain on a clean piece of paper, and dish in a circle round some well-mashed potatoes, or green peas. If you have any carrots cut them into small squares, boil them till they are tender, drain off the water, then put a teaspoonful of butter and some chopped parsley with them. Place them in the centre of the cutlets, the mashed potatoes round the carrots, the outlets on their heads round the potato. Some brown sauce round the dish, but not poured over everything.

MILLER BROTHERS

(Of LIVERPOOL)
LIMITED

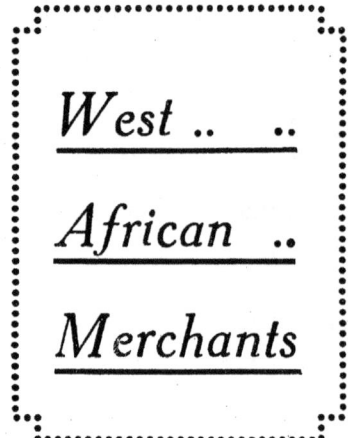

West African Merchants

Also Agents for - - Poulton & Noel's Provisions, etc.

21, WATER STREET,
LIVERPOOL

———and———

NIGERIA, WEST AFRICA

MUTTON HOT-POT.

Remarks—For this it is best to get the best end of neck of mutton, the same as for cutlets.

Best end of neck of mutton.
Some potatoes (or yams).
2 small or 1 large onion.
Pepper and salt.
1 breakfast cup of stock.

Cut the meat from the bones, keeping it as much like the shape of a cutlet as possible. Half boil the potatoes and onion. Get a fire-proof dish or a native pot, put a layer of sliced potatoes at the bottom, sprinkle with onion, pepper and salt. Lay on these half the meat, add another layer of potatoes, an onion, the rest of the meat put upon these, pour in the stock, and on the top of all put small potatoes (whole). Put the lid on the pot and bake till the top potatoes are quite soft and done. Serve in the dish in which it is cooked.

Don'ts—Don't throw away the bones and trimmings of meat. Put them in a saucepan, with a little salt, cover with water, and let them cook slowly for 2 hours. They will make a good stock.

RICE CUTLETS.

1 teacup of rice.
1 breakfastcup of cold meat.
1 onion.
A little salt and pepper.
teacup of suet.
2 tablespoons of breadcrumbs.

Wash the rice and boil it, i.e., throw it into boiling water and let it jump up and down hard for 10 or 20 minutes (10 minutes is enough for native rice). Boil the onion and chop it up fine. Chop the meat and suet very small. Strain the rice when it is cooked, and add the meat and suet to it, also the breadcrumbs and onion. Sprinkle a little salt and pepper over it. Mix all well together with a little warm stock, and cook it for a few minutes to make it into a paste.

Turn it out on to a plate to set and get cool. Cut it into the shape of a cutlet. Cover each cutlet with egg and breadcrumbs and fry in hot fat. Arrange some mashed potatoes or cooked peas in the centre of dish and the cutlets round them.

SPAGHETTI AND GRAVY.

Remarks—This makes an excellent light luncheon dish, or vegetarian dish.

Half a small pie dish of spaghetti.
1 breakfastcup of gravy.
2 tablespoons of grated Cheddar cheese.
2 tablespoons of tomato sauce or a few small tomatoes.
1 teaspoonful of butter.

The Gravy—Have this made beforehand. Keep back a little of the soup stock from the previous night, flavour it with a little Worcester or other sauce, pepper and salt. Or, if you have no stock, put a little butter or dripping at the bottom of a saucepan, shred a little onion into it and keep it moving about till the flavour is extracted, but don't let the onion burn. Then stir in a teaspoonful of flour and mix till smooth; then pour in a little water gradually; stir well so that the mixture is not lumpy; let it boil over the fire and continue to add water till you think you have enough gravy; flavour with a little Oxo, or sauce, salt and pepper.

Blanch some spaghetti; that is, throw it into a saucepan of boiling water and let it cook for five minutes. Drain dry. Then place in a clean stewpan and cover with the gravy. Let it simmer gently for three-quarters of an hour, when the gravy should be nearly all absorbed. Stir in the cheese, the butter and the tomato sauce. Serve very hot in a vegetable dish, with grated cheese sprinkled over the top. Let it brown in the oven before sending it to table.

STEWED KIDNEYS.

3 sheep's kidneys.
1 tablespoon of butter.
1 teaspoon of chopped parsley, if possible.
1 tablespoon of ketchup or A1 sauce.
1 tablespoon of flour.
1 small onion.
1 breakfast cup of stock.
Some pepper and salt.
Small squares of fried bread.

Skin the kidneys and cut in halves. Fry them in the butter for five minutes. Put the flour into a small basin, add a little stock to mix it smooth. Then add this (flour and stock), also the pepper, salt, ketchup, finely chopped onion, and the rest of the stock to the butter and kidneys. Let it simmer for 20 minutes, till the kidneys are cooked through and the gravy is nice and thick. Just before serving add the parsley, if you have any. Serve on a hot dish with the sippets of fried bread round.

STUFFED ONIONS.

A large "Kano" onion or two small ones.
1 tablespoon of minced meat or fowl.
1 teaspoon butter or dripping.
1 tablespoon breadcrumbs.
A pinch of salt and pepper.

Wash the onions, peel off the outside skin and cut a small slice off the top. Put them in a saucepan and cover them with water. Let the water come to the boil and then pull the pot on one side so that they simmer slowly. When they are tender, but not quite cooked, take them out. Scoop out some of the inside, put that on one side to be chopped up with the meat. Use the outside skin of the onion for one case, and the skin next to it, if you can get it out whole, for another case. If you use small onions, the outside skin of each will make cases. Mince your meat, put it in a basin with the breadcrumbs, the insides of the onion, salt, pepper, and butter, and if not moist enough add a little stock or gravy, or an egg beaten up. Put this mixture into the onion skins, sprinkle some bread crumbs on the top and put them in the oven for about ten minutes with a little piece of butter on the top of each. If you have a nice brown gravy, this can be served with them.

STUFFED TOMATOES.

Remarks—If possible choose tomatoes that match in shape and size if you want the dish to look well.

5 even-sized tomatoes.
3 tablespoons of any cold meat or fowl.
½ a small onion.
1 teaspoon of chopped parsley if possible.
A little gravy or sauce.
Salt and pepper.
A teaspoon of browned crumbs.

Take away all skin and bone from the meat. Chop it very finely; also the parsley and onion. Put the meat, parsley and onion into a small saucepan and add enough gravy to make it soft and creamy.

With a sharp knife cut a round piece from the stalk end of each tomato, and with the handle of a spoon scoop out the inside, taking care not to break the skin.

Add the inside of the tomato to the mixture. Stir it over the fire for two minutes. Then refill the tomatoes, heaping the mixture up slightly. Sprinkle the bread crumbs over the top. Put the tomatoes on a tin in the oven, and bake them till they are just tender. Cut some small rounds of bread, fry them, and place a tomato on each piece.

TIMBALE OF CHICKEN.

A cupful (breakfast) of macaroni.
The meat off a cold fowl.
2 tablespoons of ham if possible.
1 egg.
4 tablespoons of milk.
1 teacup of breadcrumbs.
A little pepper and salt.
A teaspoon of ketchup or sauce.

Break the macaroni into sizes the length of your middle finger. Throw it into boiling water and when it is quite tender drain off the water. Line a basin or mould with it. (A plain mould.) Chop or mince the chicken and ham—put it into a mixing basin. Add the bread crumbs, salt, pepper. Beat up the egg with the milk and sauce—pour this over the mixture and mix all thoroughly. The mixture should be moist. Put it carefully into the basin that is lined with the macaroni. Cover it with your pudding cloth, or a piece of buttered paper and steam it for 1 hour.

Don'ts—Do not let the water come over the top of the basin when you steam it and see that the water boils all the time.

CLOTHES

in the best tradition of West-End Tailoring

Clothes grave or gay, clothes discreet or lighthearted.

Your taste, your mood, your figure will be fitted perfectly at the Kingsway Stores. And in material and cut your clothes will be in the best tradition of West-End Tailoring.

KINGSWAY STORES

Branches throughout Nigeria.

VEGETABLES

HINTS ON COOKING VEGETABLES.

Remember all green vegetables, except spinach, are cooked with the lid off the saucepan. Vegetables of strong flavour, which include most green vegetables, should be well covered with fast boiling water and cooked rather quickly till done. Old potatoes and Jerusalem artichokes are put into cold water. All vegetables should be well drained after cooking, whether they are to be served with sauce or not.

FRENCH BEANS.

Remarks—These grow well in the country as a rule and if cooked well are a great acquisition.

Wash the beans well first. Then with a knife cut through the stalk end and pull off with it the stringy piece down the back. Do the same with the stringy piece on the other side. Now slice them very fine and in a slanting direction. Have ready a saucepan of boiling water, put a spoonful of salt in it, and then throw in the sliced beans. Boil quickly till they are tender, then drain them in a colander if you have one. Throw away the water. Return the beans to the saucepan. Dust them with salt and pepper and add a small piece of butter. Shake them about in this till the butter is melted. Serve very hot.

HARICOT BEANS.

Soak the beans in cold water for at least three hours. Then have ready a saucepan of boiling water and put in the beans and let them cook gently till they are tender. Do not put salt in the water, but cook them for about two or three hours very gently. Strain off the water. Put a, little butter and some salt and pepper in the saucepan, toss the beans in this and serve them hot.

TO BOIL CABBAGE.

Take off the coarse and damaged outer leaves. Then put the "heart" and tender leaves into a basin of cold water with a good spoonful of salt. This will draw out any insects. Throw away this water after a time and soak the cabbage again in clean water. Then have ready a saucepan of boiling water and put in the cabbage with some salt. Let it boil quickly with the lid off the pot. When the stalks are tender the cabbage is done. Throw away the water and strain the cabbage well, pressing it with the bottom part of an old saucer to get all the water away.

CARROTS.

Carrots should always be scraped with a knife and not peeled. Wash them well and put them into a saucepan of boiling water and salt. Boil, according to their, size, from 20 minutes to one hour. If the carrots are to be served with boiled meat they can be cooked with it and not separately.

LENTIL CAKES.

Remarks—A vegetarian dish which makes a pleasant change as a breakfast or lunch dish.

A breakfast cup of red lentils.
1 onion.
4 tablespoons of breadcrumbs.
2 eggs.
Some pepper and salt.
Some fat or oil for frying.

It is not necessary to soak the lentils over night, but this is often done. They must, however, be washed first in two or three changes of water. Half fill a small saucepan with boiling water, put in the lentils and the onion cut in halves. Let the lentils boil gently till they are soft and have taken up nearly all the water. They will take about one hour. Now break the egg into a cup and beat it for a minute with a fork. Then put the lentils into a basin (they should be like a purée, thick and moist), add nearly all the bread-crumbs, the pepper, salt and egg, and mix all well together. Then take out a spoonful and make it into a small cake like a fish cake. Break the other egg on to a plate, dip the cakes into it, then sprinkle with the rest of the bread crumbs and fry them as you fry fish cakes.

Don'ts—Don't let the lentils be wet and sloppy when you put them into the basin, they must be rather firm like meat when it has been minced. If the lentils seem lumpy, don't forget they can be rubbed through a sieve, but if boiled gently a long time this is not necessary.

MASHED POTATOES.

7 or 8 potatoes.
1 tablespoon of butter or dripping.
Some salt and pepper.
1 tablespoon of milk.

Peel the potatoes, put them in a saucepan and cover them with cold water. Add the salt. When they are soft drain off the water and let them steam on one side of the fire. Then with a fork or wooden spoon, or the end of a rolling-pin mash them up till there are no lumps. They can be mashed quite well in the saucepan in which they are boiled. Add the butter, milk and pepper, and beat them light and creamy with a fork. Heap them up on a vegetable dish tidily. When you have mashed the potatoes, make them up into balls. Brush them over with an egg beaten up. Place them on a greased tin and bake them a nice brown.

STEWED ONIONS WITH WHITE SAUCE.

5 or 6 plain boiled onions.
1 tablespoon of butter or margarine.
½ tablespoon of flour.
1 teacup of milk and water.
Some salt and pepper.

Make a white sauce thus: Melt the butter in a saucepan, stir in the flour, then add the milk—a little to begin with till you have no lumps in the flour— then add the rest. Stir well all the time till it thickens. Now boil the onions in this for five minutes and serve hot.

PAW-PAW.

Paw-paw must be picked green if used as a vegetable.

Peel the paw-paw and take out the seeds. Then cut the rest up into pieces about the size of match box. Have ready a saucepan of boiling water, throw in the pieces of paw-paw. Add some salt and let it all cook gently till soft. Drain away the water, place the pieces of paw-paw on a vegetable dish, sprinkle a. little pepper over them and cover with a white sauce if possible. It is not unlike vegetable marrow cooked in this way. Paw-paw is also very good stuffed with mince and covered with white sauce or it can be fried.

TO BOIL POTATOES.

Potatoes.
Enough water to cover them.
Salt.

Peel the potatoes very thinly and if the potatoes are old put them into cold water with a teaspoonful of salt. Bring gently to the boil. When you can pierce them easily with a fork, pour off the water, keep the lid off the pot, draw it to one side of the fire and let them steam. As a rule native cooks do not boil them long enough and do not let them "steam" when cooked. They serve them looking sodden and dull and a bad colour.

NEW POTATOES.

These should be scraped, not peeled, and put straight into boiling water with a little mint, if you have any, and some salt. Then, when cooked, steamed in the same way as old potatoes.

POTATO CAKES.

5 or 6 cold boiled potatoes.
1 tablespoon of butter.
1 tablespoon of milk.
1 tablespoon of grated cheese.
Some pepper and salt.

Mash the cold potatoes till there are no lumps. Add the butter melted, the milk and the pepper and salt. Stir in the cheese. Grease a tin. Turn the potato mixture in a neat heap like a cake on to the tin, mark it roughly with a fork. Heat and brown in the oven, then slip it on to a vegetable dish, or make the mixture into small round cakes.

Telephone: 116, LAGOS.   Telegrams: "TAN LAGOS."

Tin Areas of Nigeria
―――― LIMITED, ――――

MARINA, LAGOS.

Registered Offices:
1-4, Giltspur Street - - - London

HIGH - CLASS
PROVISIONS

Large and Varied Stocks
.. .. carried at .. ..
ZARIA, JOS, BUKURU

BRANCHES at Abeokuta, Ibadan, Kano, Katerigi, Katcha, Minna, Lokoja, Onitsha, Ibi and ACCRA.

POTATO CHIPS.

A few potatoes.
Salt and pepper.
1 tablespoon or more of dripping for frying.

Peel and wash the potatoes, then cut them across in very thin slices and fry in smoking fat. Turn them on to clean paper to dry and dust them with salt and pepper. They should be served very hot, and must be dry and chippy, not sodden and greasy. A favourite "gadget" or "small chop" dish.

POTATOES A LA MAITRE D'HOTEL.

Slices of cold potato.
1 tablespoon of butter.
1 tablespoon of flour.
1 teacup of milk and water.
Some pepper and salt.
Chopped parsley, if possible.

If you have any cold boiled potatoes left over, cut them into round slices, not too thin. Then make a sauce, thus:—Melt the butter in a saucepan, Stir in the flour, add a little milk and water, stir well till it is smooth, then add the rest of the milk and stir while it boils and thickens. Add the pepper, salt and parsley, and then let the potatoes heat in this sauce.

POTATO RIBBONS.

Peel and wash the potatoes, which should not be too small. Cut them across in thick slices. Then peel each slice very thinly, as you take the rind off an apple. Peel round and round, and the thinner the slice the less chance of it snapping in two. It is not easy to do, and wants care. Tie these ribbons of potato lightly into knots and fry in smoking fat for a few seconds. Drain them on kitchen paper and dust with salt and pepper. Serve very hot. This is rather a wasteful but effective way of doing potatoes—when potatoes are scarce.

SAUTE POTATOES.

A few nice-sized potatoes.
2 tablespoons of butter or dripping.
Some salt and pepper.

Peel and wash the potatoes, cut them into chunks the length of the potato. Put these into cold water and bring them gently to the boil, and when they are soft pour off the water and empty the potatoes on to a clean cloth to dry. Let the dripping or butter get hot in a stewpan and toss the potatoes in. When brown on all sides take them out and drain them on clean paper. Dust them with salt and pepper.

SPINACH.

Remarks—This boils down so much that quite a quantity is necessary to make a good-sized dish.

Pull off the outside leaves and large stalks and wash the tender leaves in cold water—three or four changes of water. Now put in a saucepan without any water and sprinkle with salt. There is so much moisture in spinach that it does not require to be cooked in water. Keep the lid on the pot while it cooks. Stir it frequently. When tender strain it through a colander, if you have one, and squeeze the moisture out with the back of any old saucer. Chop it very finely, or pass it through a wire sieve. Return it to the saucepan with a little pepper and butter, or a spoonful of milk, and mix well. Serve it in a "mound" shape on a dish with small pieces of fried bread round it; or serve it on squares of toast with a poached egg on each square.

SPINACH EGGS.

Some cooked spinach.
Four small boiled eggs.

Place the spinach when cooked as in previous recipe on a dish in the shape of a bird's nest, putting in the middle, four small lightly boiled eggs, with the shells off them.

TURNIPS.

Remarks—Turnips are most appetizing if mashed.

Cut off the thick rind, and put them in boiling water with salt. Boil till quite soft, for about 20 to 30 minutes. When they are ready, strain off the water and pass them through a wire sieve, or beat them with a fork. Add a small piece of butter, some salt and pepper, and put them in a clean saucepan and beat them lightly with a fork.

THERE IS SATISFACTION IN "WALTON TROPICAL CLOTHING"

Gentlemen going Overseas can obtain reliable Clothing and Equipment at Walton's in up-to-date styles and at economical prices.
The Tailoring imparted into Tussore and Palm Beach materials is of a high standard, and materials are selected for long service.
Suitable Shirts, Underwear, Boots, Trunks, etc., are available, and shopping for Overseas is made easy. For satisfaction—Outfit at Walton's

THE ABOVE CLOTHING READY TO WEAR

Can be made to measure if necessary at slightly extra cost

A few selected items from our List:

Tussore Jacket and Trousers ..	25/-, 42/-
Cream Gabardine Jacket and Trousers	30/-, 42/-
White Drill Jackets and Trousers	21/-, 29/6
Khaki ,, ,, ,, ..	21/-, 29/6
Palm Beach ,, ,, ,, ..	44/6, 50/-
Wool Solaro ,, ,, ,, ..	.. 85/-
White or Khaki Drill Trousers ..	.. 11/9
Bush Shirts	.. 8/11
Drill Shorts	.. 6/6
Spine Pads	.. 1/11
Calvin Cord Riding Breeches ..	.. 21/-
Khaki and Drab Drill Riding Breeches	15/6, 18/11
White Drill Dinner Jackets ..	.. 18/6
,, ,, Mess ,, ..	.. 16/6
Tropical Weatherproofs.. ..	63/-, 84/-
Waterproof guaranteed all climates	.. 49/6
30-in. Airtight Case West African Box ..	42/-, 50/-
Cork and Rubber Helmets, Gents'	16/6, 18/6
Pith Helmets, Gents'	.. 18/6
Wolsey Helmet	16/6, 25/-
Colonial Felts, all Fur	.. 21/-
Mosquito Boots, White Canvas ..	.. 19/6
Mosquito Boots, best quality Black Glacé ..	27/6
Mosquito Boots, best quality Brown Sheepskin	27/6
Airtight Boxes, Wardrobe Trunks, Cabin Trunks, Mosquito Nets, Camp Equipment ..	—
Ladies' Mosquito Boots 18/11, 25/-,	42/-
Helmets, Ladies' Cork and Pith	.. 18/6
Ladies' Tropical Raincoats ..	.. 59/6
Ladies' Tussore Dustcoats ..	.. 35/-
Ladies' Riding Breeches, Mosquito Boots, Helmets and Sunshades a speciality	—
Children's Cork Helmets ..	.. 10/6

Customers tell us it is surprising that we can impart so much style into washing suits. We have a range of specially selected cloths, and claim to offer the finest possible value.

SERVICE KIT · **MINING KIT** · **BUSH KIT**

Isaac Walton & Co Ltd

CITY ESTABLISHMENT:
1 to 9 LUDGATE HILL, LONDON, E.C. 4
Also YORK, AND NEWCASTLE-ON-TYNE

MEAT.

RULES FOR ROASTING BEEF OR MUTTON.

Allow ¼ hour to every pound. Most joints in Nigeria are very small, weighing between 2 to 4 lbs. ¾ hour to 1 hour is nearly always sufficient. This is a rough guide.

If there does not seem much fat on the joint add 2 spoons of dripping and place it on the meat. Baste well—this is very important To "baste" is to pour over the joint at intervals some of the hot dripping that is in the oven dish. This keeps the joint moist, prevents it from shrivelling up into a dried piece of hard meat with no goodness in it. It is a good plan to always have a small tin of water in the oven to keep the air moist.

Don'ts—Do not put the joint into a cold oven; have it nearly as hot as you want it for pastry before you put the joint in.

TO MAKE THE GRAVY.

Lift the meat from the tin, pour off the fat into a basin, leaving the dregs in the tin. Put this on the fire, shake over it a spoonful of flour, add 1 cup of water, a pinch of salt, teaspoon of browning. Stir over the fire till it thickens, then pour it into a sauceboat.

STEWING.

To stew is to cook very slowly, with very little liquor. Inferior parts of meat may be rendered digestible and palatable by this way of cooking.

The best way is to put the meat to be cooked into a jar with a lid. Place the jar in a saucepan of boiling water. Cooking in this way prevents the contents of the jar from reaching boiling point This is important, as meat boiled is hardened.

TO BROIL CHOPS AND STEAKS.

Have a clear fire, one that is not smoking. Grease the bars of the broiler, or if you have no broiler grease a frying-pan. Rub the chops or steak with a little butter or ground-nut oil, pepper and salt Broil quickly; do not turn too often. Chops take about 7 minutes. Steak takes about 10 minutes, according to the thickness. All the juices are kept in by cooking this way.

TO BOIL A HAM.

The hams are generally preserved and packed in salt. Soak the ham in a large basin: of water for at least a whole day. Change the water three times. To soak it longer than one day will not spoil it. A very clean petrol tin makes a good cooking pot for a ham. The rule is hour to the pound—a ham generally takes 3 to 4 hours to boil. If a cupful of vinegar and § cloves are added to the boiling water it improves the flavour of the ham, but this is not necessary.

Don'ts—Don't take the ham out of the water when it is boiled. Leave it in the pot all night, it improves the flavour. It will skin easily when cold; the skin should peel off easily. Dust the top with sifted brown bread crumbs or biscuit crumbs.

BEEF ROLL.

Remarks—This is a very good cold lunch dish, with salad, and is not difficult to make. It is a good way of using up the end of a ham or piece of bacon. It looks well if it can be glazed, but as gelatine is not easy to get the roll can be made to look quite appetizing if decorated with small sprigs of parsley, or lettuce and tomatoes.

A piece of beefsteak (about 1s. 3d. worth).
The same quantity of ham (the last pieces off a ham bone).

1 teacup of fresh breadcrumbs (not dried in the oven).
2 eggs.
A little grated nutmeg.
Some salt and pepper.
A pudding cloth, quite clean, and some string.

Mince the steak raw, and the ham or bacon. Put them in a large basin. Add the breadcrumbs, pepper, salt and nutmeg. Put the eggs one by one in a cup and beat them. Mix them with the meat, and if the eggs are very small you will probably want three. When it is all well mixed, turn the mixture on to a board and roll it into the shape of a good healthy sausage.

Take your pudding-cloth by the four corners, and dip the middle part into the kettle of boiling water; open it out, shake some flour over the wet part, then place the roll in the middle of the cloth. Fold it round the sausage. Tie the corners tightly with a piece of string, carrying one end of the string right across to tie the other end. This makes a kind of handle to lower the roll into the water and to pull it out again. Nip the centre of the cloth together with a pin.

Have ready a large pot of boiling water, put an old saucer or plate at the bottom, drop in the roll carefully and let it boil 3 hours. If you have some gelatine make a glaze and pour it over the roll when it is cold.

Don'ts—Don't tie up too loosely. Don't let the water boil away, keep a kettle at the side and fill up the pot as it empties.

Don't let the water stop jumping, or "get off the boil," after the roll is once in.

Compagnie Francaise
DE
l'Afrique Occidentale

Société anonyme au
Capital de 25 Millions de Francs.

GENERAL MERCHANTS.

Head Office:

32, Cours Pierre-Puget, MARSEILLE.

Branches at

PARIS: 58, Rue Saint-Lazare.
BORDEAUX: 73, Cours Pasteur.
LIVERPOOL: Royal Liver Building.
MANCHESTER: 75, Whitworth Street.

NIGERIAN BRANCHES:

LAGOS, KANO, PORT HARCOURT, IBADAN, ABEOKUTA, ZARIA, OSHOGBO.

GATEAU OF COLD MEAT.

A breakfast cup of minced meat.
½ teacup of breadcrumbs.
1 tablespoonful (or more) of gravy or stock.
A tablespoonful of fresh breadcrumbs.
1 egg.
A little chopped onion.
A little pepper and salt
A mould or small plain basin.

Grease a mould or basin and sprinkle the inside well with breadcrumbs. Mince the meat; put it into a basin, and add the onion, pepper and salt, the gravy and breadcrumbs. Mix with one egg. Turn the mixture into the mould and bake it for 20 minutes. Turn it out when it is cold.

PRESSED HUMP.

Remarks—This is an excellent cold dish for lunch, with salad, if the ingredients for the "pickle" are obtainable.

Prepare a pickle as described in "Pickle for Meat". Place the hump in the pickle and keep it there for about three days. Look at it every day and turn it over. Then take it out and soak it well for about 9 hours, say from about 9 a.m. to 6 p.m. When you take it out of the water in which it has been soaked, place it at once in a stew-pot and just cover it with cold water. Put it over the fire and let it come to the boil. When the water begins to jump draw the stew-pan to one side of the fire and let it cook slowly and gently for about half an hour. A good rule to follow is: Allow 20 minutes' cooking to every pound of meat.

Now take it out of the stew-pan, place it at once on a plate or dish, place another plate on the top, the right side of the plate touching the meat, then on the top of this plate place a heavy weight—a large stone, or piece of iron. When the meat is cold trim the rough edges and decorate the dish and the meat with parsley, or lettuce and tomatoes. If you want it to look really finished, glaze the top in the same way as described for Beef Roll (see page 96).

Don'ts—Don't put the hump into boiling water to save time! It must be put into cold and then brought to the boil.

STEWED HUMP.

Wash the hump when it comes from the market, then place it in a stewpan, just cover it with cold water and place it over the fire. If you have any vegetables, such as carrots, turnips, onions, prepare a few and put them also in the stewpan. Add some salt and 4 or 5 cloves. When the water begins to jump draw the pan away from the fire and let the meat then simmer and cook slowly. About half an hour should be sufficient, but the time depends on the weight of the hump (20 minutes to each pound). Take out the hump and put on a plate to get cold. If the vegetables are not cooked enough put the pan over the fire till they are tender. Hump is nicer eaten cold than hot.

Don't—Do not forget the hump must first be put into cold water, not into hot.

LIVER AND BACON.

Remarks—This dish can be very unappetizing, but it need not be. It wants very careful cooking.

A little liver.
About 4 slices of thinly cut frying bacon.
1 tablespoons of flour.
½ an onion.
A teacup of stock or soup left over from dinner.

Cut the bacon into thin slices, take off the rind. Place the slices in a frying pan but do not put them on the fire yet till you have prepared the liver. Wash the liver and dry it with a clean kitchen cloth, cut it into slices about the size of a small biscuit. Now put 1 spoonful of flour on to a plate with some pepper and salt. Dip each piece of liver into it. Let the frying pan get hot. Fry the bacon—turning it once. Put it on a hot dish. Now put the liver in the pan, a few pieces at a time as they must not get on top of each other. Fry it well and cut one slice to see if it is cooked. It will look red inside if it is not done enough. When it is ready, place it on the dish neatly with the bacon. Slice the onion and let it fry and add it to the dish. Now make the gravy. Stir the other spoon of flour into the frying pan, when it is brown add the stock and stir it round and round till it boils and gets thick. Pour this sauce over the liver in the middle of the dish.

Don'ts—Don't let the liver look pale and uncooked; it should be firm and brown; but not burnt.

MEAT PASTIES.

Remarks—These make a nice change for lunch, also to take with one on a journey.

Pasty.

A breakfast cup of minced meat.
Half an onion.
Some pepper and salt.
A tablespoon of water.
A very little nutmeg, grated.
A teaspoon of butter or dripping.

Mince the meat. Put the butter in a saucepan and let it melt. Then cut up the onion and let it frizzle in the butter for a minute or two. Then put in the meat, water, pepper and salt, nutmeg, and half a teaspoon of Worcester sauce if liked. Stir all together, and while it is slowly cooking on the side of the fire make the pastry.

The Pastry.

1 breakfast cup of flour.
3 tablespoons of dripping.
½ teaspoon of baking powder.

1 teacup of water.
A little salt.
A mixing basin.
Flour board and rolling pin or clean glass bottle.

See that your hands are clean. Have everything you want on the table before you begin. Put the flour in the basin, mix in the baking powder and salt, then rub in the dripping with the tips of your fingers. Add half the teacup of water and mix well with a fork; if too stiff add a little more water, but don't slop a lot in. You may want the whole cupful, you may not want so much, so don't put it all in at first.

The pastry, when well mixed, should roll into a ball and come clean away from the sides of the basin. Flour the pastry board, turn the pastry on to it in a nice round lump, and sprinkle a little flour over it, also on the rolling pin. Roll out the pastry; roll away from you all the time, not backwards and forwards. Turn the pastry round and roll again. If it sticks to the board a little lift it up and sprinkle flour underneath. Roll it into a nice shape, not too thin. Then cut the pastry into large rounds, as big as the top of a breakfast cup. When you have cut out as many as you can, roll up the bits that are left, flour it a little, and roll out again. Cut more rounds. Do this till you have used up all the pastry you can. Now take the saucepan off the fire. Put a teaspoon of the mince on one side of the round and fold the other over it; wet the edge with a feather dipped in water to make them stick together. Press them with your linger so that the mince will not come out in the baking. Bake in a quick or hot oven about 20 minutes. If you brush them over with an egg it will make them look shiny and glazed and more "high class."

Another way to do them, if you have patty pans: Cut rounds a little larger than the patty pans, two rounds for each pan. Put one round on the patty pan, put a teaspoonful of mince in the centre, then cover this with the other round. Wet the lower edge to make the edges stick together. Make one hole at the top with a sharp piece of match-stick, or make holes with the fork. This is to let the steam get away, and bad gases.

MEAT PIE.

A large piece of steak.
2 kidneys, if possible.
2 eggs.

Boil the eggs hard, dip them in cold water to prevent them going green, shell them, and cut them in fours. Cut the steak into thin pieces and roll them up with a piece of kidney inside each. Put 1 teaspoon of flour, 1 teaspoon of salt, and teaspoon of pepper on to a plate, mix them together and dip each piece of meat into it. Arrange these rolls of meat and kidney in a pie-dish and fill up the dish nearly to the top with water.

For the Pastry.

4 breakfast cups of flour.
2 large tablespoons of dripping or margarine.
1 teaspoon of baking powder.
A little salt and pepper.
A teacup of cold water.
Pie-dish and egg-cup.

Have clean hands and see that everything you want is on the table beside you—pastry board, rolling-pin, etc. Put the flour into a basin and mix the baking powder and salt in it. Then rub in the dripping with the ends of your fingers. If it is too hard shave it thin with a knife, then rub it in. Add the water—about half the cupful at first, then any more you may want put in carefully so as not to put in too much. Mix with a fork or knife into a stiff paste. It must not be wet and sticky, but come away from the sides of the basin quite cleanly.

PEOPLE *who* KNOW
ALWAYS USE
POULTON & NOEL'S
— ENGLISH —
Preserved Provisions

P. & N's Meat and Fish Paste excellent.
P. & N's Puddings in Tins (large variety).

OX TONGUES, ENTREES, GALANTINES.
——— All Recommended. ———

POULTON & NOEL, LTD., LONDON, N.7., ENGLAND
INDENTS RECEIVED THROUGH EUROPEAN EXPORT HOUSES ONLY.

Now put an egg-cup turned upside down in the middle of the pie-dish. See that the meat is arranged nicely in the dish, the water for the gravy poured in, and the pieces of egg placed nicely on the top. Then flour a board, turn the pastry on to it, sprinkle a little flour on to it and on to the rolling-pin, then roll the pastry out rather larger than the pie-dish.

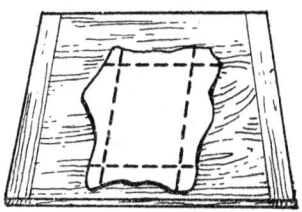

Cut the rough outside edges off. Wet the edge of the dish with a feather dipped in water and put the strip of pastry round the edge, the tidy cut edge outside, the uneven edge inside. Wet the edge again and lay the rest of the pastry over the pie. Hold up the dish and with a sharp knife cut off the ragged edges. Make a few holes in the pastry with a fork to let the steam and gases out. With the pieces of pastry over decorate the top of the pie. Mark round the edges of the pie with the handle-end of the fork. Bake the pie for 4 hours. If the pastry seems as if it would burn, cover it with a piece of paper.

To make Ornaments for the Pie.

A Rose for the Middle.
Roll out the pieces of pastry that are over. Cut a long strip about as wide across as the blade of a knife. Roll it up, pinch one end in your fingers, and with a knife cut the other end across and across.

Then turn back each little separate piece. Stick this rose in the centre.

The Leaves.

Cut another long strip about the width of the knife-blade, then cut it slanting. Press each piece gently with the back of a knife to make the marks as on a leaf.

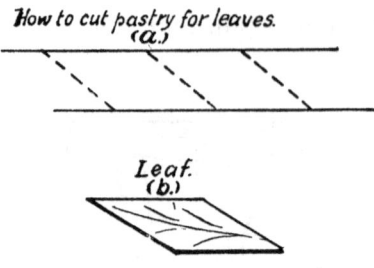

Arrange these on the top of the pie. Brush the whole of the top with the yolk of egg and the pie will then look glazed when quite baked. If eggs are scarce this is not necessary, a little milk and water will do nearly as well.

To Bake.

Bake pie in a quick oven for the first 20 minutes, to make the pastry light. Then cook slowly, to cook the meat through and keep it tender. 4 to 2 hours is necessary. When the pastry is done it is a good plan to cover it with greased paper—greased side not on the pastry. This will prevent the pastry getting too brown, or burning.

Don'ts—Don't forget to make the holes with a fork in the top of the pie, or a slit with a, knife near where you put on the leaves.

POTATO PIE.

1 breakfast cup or more of minced meat.
5 or 6 good-sized potatoes, or some yam.
1 tablespoon of dripping.
1 tablespoon of milk.

Some salt and pepper.
1 teaspoon of sauce.
A teaspoon of onion, chopped fine.
½ teacup of stock.

Peel the potatoes, put them in a saucepan, cover them with cold water and let them boil till they are soft. Drain off the water and mash them with a wooden spoon or beat them with a 'fork. Put the dripping and milk, pepper and salt on to them, and beat all together till they are creamy and soft. Mince the meat and put in a pie-dish. Shake some flour over it, a little pepper, salt, the sauce and the stock. Spread the potatoes over the top and mark neatly with a fork. Bake in a quick oven for hour.

Don'ts—Don't leave any lumps in the potatoes, beat them till they look white and creamy. Don't leave skin or fat in the meat.

A GOOD STEW.

5 or 6 large potatoes (or some yam.)
½ tea cup of pearl barley.
2 large onions or 4 small ones.
A fowl or some steak or remains of joint.
2 large cups of water.
Some salt and pepper.

Wash the potatoes and peel them. Wash the onions and take off the outside skin. Put 2 cups of water into a large saucepan and make it boil. Then throw in the barley and the onion. If after a time there does not seem enough water, add some more. When the barley has swelled and is soft, put in the potatoes (they do not take as long to cook as the barley so must not go in with it, or they would boil away). Then joint the fowl or cut the steak into small pieces and add that to the saucepan. Now let all stew gently for an hour.

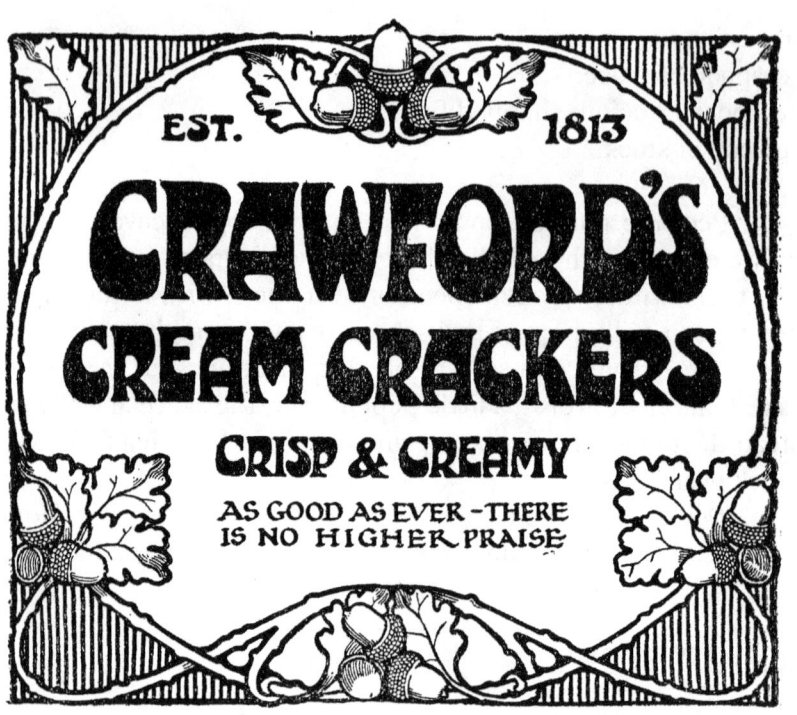

EST. 1813
CRAWFORD'S CREAM CRACKERS
CRISP & CREAMY
AS GOOD AS EVER – THERE IS NO HIGHER PRAISE

Specially packed for Export.

Cadbury's
Cocoa and Chocolates

"The very finest products."—Med.Mag.

MADE AT BOURNVILLE

Cadbury, Bournville, Eng.

Don'ts—Don't put in cooked meat till about half an hour before the stew is served, and don't let it boil or it will be hard and tough; draw the saucepan on to one side. Cooked meat only wants to be thoroughly warmed through when added to a stew.

TOAD-IN-THE-HOLE.

1 tin of sausages.
1 breakfast cup of flour.
2 eggs.
2 breakfast cups of milk. (If Ideal milk, add cupful of water.)

Put the flour in a basin; make a hole in the centre. Break one egg into a cup—if the egg is good pour it into the hole. Try the other egg first in the cup, and if good, add it to the first egg. Add half the milk and beat all together for 5 minutes with a wooden spoon. Add the rest of the milk. Let it stand one hour. Grease a pie dish—or a baking tin. (A pie dish is better.) Cut the sausages in half and arrange them in the dish. Sprinkle over them a little pepper and salt. Pour the batter over the sausages and bake in a nice hot oven for nearly an hour. Pieces of lean meat cut into neat squares will do instead of sausages— but the latter are more tasty.

PUDDINGS, PASTRY AND SWEETS

HINTS ON MAKING PUDDINGS.

1. Before putting milk into a pan to boil, put a little cold water into the pan first. Bring to the boil and then add the milk. This prevents the milk catching.
2. To prevent milk running over when it comes to the boil put a spoon in.
3. Batter puddings need a quick oven.
4. Puddings made mostly of milk and eggs should be gently cooked as a strong heat will make them curdle.
5. When beating the whites of eggs add a tiny pinch of salt. This will make them froth quicker as well as stiffen them.
6. Always break eggs one by one into a cup or basin first to see if they are good, before adding them to the flour, etc.

USEFUL HINTS ABOUT PASTRY.

1. Make it in as cool a place as possible.
2. Use good flour, good dripping or lard and eggs.
3. Use a clean board and rolling pin, and have clean hands.
4. Add the water rather freely at first to the flour when beginning to mix, but with care and caution at the end.
5. It is best to mix all the dry ingredients together first, then add the liquids.
6. Make it as quickly as possible and if it contains baking powder put it in the oven as soon as possible.
7. Have a quick oven for pastry.

Don'ts—

1. Don't rub or roll the butter into the flour heavily.
2. Don't put in too much water.

3. Don't sprinkle too much flour on the board or rolling pin, just enough to prevent the pastry sticking to either.
4. Don't roll heavily or unevenly, try to roll always one way.
5. Don't put the pastry in a cool oven. Don't put it at once into a cold place, after baking—place it where it will gradually cool.

If the pastry is hard or tough, probably your oven was not quite hot or "quick" enough; or you did not use quite enough fat, or you used too much water.

BATTER PUDDING.

1 teacup of flour.
1 saltspoon of salt.
3 eggs.
2 breakfast cups of milk.

Put the flour into a basin and mix the salt with it. Break the eggs separately and, if good, add them to the flour and beat them well together. Add by degrees the milk, stirring all the time till the batter is mixed. Grease a pudding basin and pour the batter in. Wet your pudding cloth, that is, dip the middle into boiling water, flour the middle part and place it over the pudding and tie it with string tight round the edge. Then tie the four corners on to the top and put in a saucepan of boiling water. Let it boil for an hour and keep the lid well on. When done, turn the pudding out on to a hot dish and serve with sifted or brown sugar.

BREAD AND JAM FRITTERS.

4 tablespoons of flour.
½ breakfastcup of milk.
A pinch of salt.
1 egg.
4 thin slices of bread, spread with jam and made into sandwiches and cut diamond shape.

For the Batter—Sieve together the flour and salt into a basin. Make a hole in the middle into which break an egg. Mix it smoothly, adding gradually the milk. Beat the batter well and let it stand a. few hours. Make the jam sandwiches, not too large. Dip each one into the batter, then drop them into a frying-pan of boiling fat, and fry till a. golden brown, then drain them well on kitchen paper. Sprinkle castor sugar over them and serve.

CALIFORNIA PUDDING.

1 breakfastcup of flour.
4 tablespoons of butter or margarine.
1 teacup of treacle.
1 egg.
1 teaspoon of carbonate of soda.
1 teaspoon or more ground ginger.
A littler milk.
A pinch of salt.

Put the flour, butter and treacle into a basin. Beat it with a little milk and salt, add ground ginger to taste. Mix to a stiff batter with milk, pour into a pudding basin, cover with greased paper and tie cloth over as for beef steak pudding. Boil 4 hours. Serve with hot treacle, or melted butter.

CARAMEL PUDDING.

For the caramel:—
2 tablespoons of lump sugar.
½ teacup of cold water.

For the pudding:—
2 eggs.
1 tablespoon of castor sugar.
1 breakfast cup of milk.

Put the loaf sugar and the water into a stewpan—boil quickly until it is coffee colour— stir well and pour it quickly into a dry clean pudding basin (or plain soufflé mould) and let it coat the mould all over. Make a custard of the yolks, white of egg, the castor sugar and milk, thus— Break the eggs into a basin, add the sugar. Boil the milk and when it is a little cool pour it on to the eggs and sugar. Then strain it into the mould you have coated with the caramel. Cover it over with a piece of greased paper and put it in a saucepan of boiling water and steam very slowly for 4 hour. Turn it out on to a dish and some of the caramel will run off and form a sauce.

Don'ts—Don't let the boiling water come over the pudding.

CHOCOLATE JELLY.

1 oz. or more of Nelson's Gelatine (opaque).
1 pint of milk (two tumblerfuls).
2 tablespoons of grated chocolate or Cadbury's essence of cocoa.
4 tablespoons (small) of sugar.

Dissolve the gelatine in pint of milk and let it stand for a few hours. Mix into a smooth paste the chocolate or cocoa and sugar with cold milk. Place the gelatine with the other pint of milk on the fire and when nearly boiling add the chocolate and sugar. Let all boil together, stirring one way all the time for ten minutes. Take off the pan and put the mixture into a mould. Make it a day before it is wanted. This is very good.

JOHN HOLT & COMPANY
(LIVERPOOL) LIMITED *(Incorporated in England)*

General West African Merchants : and : Ship-Owners

HEAD OFFICE: **LAGOS:** Broad Street
Royal Liver Building   **EBUTE METTA:**
Liverpool   Denton Street

Branches in all the principal Towns and Villages in Nigeria; Also in Togoland, Dahomey, Cameroons, Spanish Guinea and French Congo.

Our Ebute Metta Branch is well-stocked with the best brands of Imported Provisions, Wines and Spirits, Household Requisites and Men's Outfitting at reasonable prices. We receive continuous supplies and our stocks are consequently fresh. All orders are executed under European supervision, and are delivered anywhere in Lagos or Ebute Metta free of charge. Up-country orders receive prompt attention and are carefully packed and put on rail free.

The Manager of our European Trade Department will be pleased to answer all enquiries. . . Please address to Ebute Metta.

We have recently opened in Lagos a Garage fully equipped with the necessary machinery for effecting repairs under skilled European supervision, to motor-cars and motor-cycles. The Garage carries large stocks of spare parts for Overland Cars.

Overland Cars, commercial motor vehicles and motor-cycles on sale. . . Motor vehicles for hire.

—— **Sole Agency for the famous Clincher Tyres.** ——

Please address all enquiries to our Motor Department, Lagos.

CHOCOLATE SOUFFLE.

Remarks—This is a very successful dinner party sweet if made with care.
3 tablespoons of chocolate powder.
1 breakfast cup of milk.
2 eggs or 3 if they are small.
2 tablespoons of castor sugar.
8 sheets of gelatine (or ¾ oz.)

Put the chocolate and milk into a small clean saucepan and cook them together. Keep them well stirred till they thicken. Then add the sugar and the yolks of the eggs. Cook a little but do not let it boil. Now take it off the fire. In another saucepan melt the gelatine in 4 a teacup of water. Then let it run through a strainer into the chocolate. Allow this to cool and when on the point of setting—fold gently into the whites of the eggs previously beaten to a stiff froth. Pour it into a china or glass mould, and when cool, turn out carefully. A pinch of salt added to the whites of the eggs will help to stiffen them. Whip them for about 15 minutes.

CORNFLOUR MOULD.

2 breakfast cups of milk.
2 tablespoons of cornflour.
1½ teaspoons of sugar.
4 or 5 drops of vanilla essence.

Put the cornflour into a basin and mix it smoothly with about a tablespoon or more of milk. Put the rest of the milk into a saucepan—let it boil and when it begins to rise take it off the fire and pour it over the cornflour stirring all the time. Pour it back into the saucepan and boil it till it gets nice and thick—then sweeten it and put in the vanilla or any other essence to taste. Wet a basin or mould, your in the cornflour and let it set. Turn out on to a glass dish when cold.

COCOA MOULD.

This is made exactly the same way—only add 1 tablespoon of grated cocoa or chocolate to the cornflour—and mix them to a paste with a little milk. Pour the boiling milk over this and carry on as with the cornflour mould.

CUSTARD—TO SERVE WITH FRUIT.

3 eggs.
1 breakfast cup of milk.
1 tablespoon of castor sugar.

Break the eggs into a basin, add the sugar—and beat them together. Put the milk in a saucepan and warm it then add it to the eggs. Stand the basin in a saucepan of boiling water. The water must only come up half-way. Stir the custard still it thickens. Then pour it into custard glasses, or over the fruit or pudding.

CUSTARD—BAKED.

Ingredients: the same as above.

Break the eggs into a basin and add the sugar. Beat the eggs just enough to mix them—then add the milk and flavouring if you want any. Grease a small pie dish. Turn the custard into this and bake for about five minutes in the oven.
Don'ts—Don't let it bake too quickly—stand it in a baking dish filled with boiling water to be on the safe side.

BAKED DUFF.

Remarks—This is the same recipe as the rock buns and plain cake—but is eaten hot and makes a very good lunch pudding.

1 breakfast cup of flour.
2 tablespoons of currants (well cleaned.)
3 tablespoons of sugar.
1 tablespoon of candied peel (can be left out.)
1 large teaspoon of baking powder.
1 salt spoon of grated nutmeg.
3 tablespoons of dripping or butter.
2 eggs.
2 tablespoons of milk and water (half and half.)
A pinch of salt.

Have everything ready before beginning. To clean the currants—shake a little flour over them, rub them well in it and then pick out stalks, etc. Put the flour into a basin, add the baking powder, salt, nutmeg and sugar. Rub in the dripping with the tips of the fingers till it all looks like breadcrumbs. Then add the candied peel (if you have any) and currants. Break the eggs and if good, beat them for a minute with a fork, add some of the milk to the eggs and pour on to the flour, etc. Mix all well together and if too dry and stiff, add the rest of the milk; but it is better not to put too much in at first. Grease a pie dish—put the mixture in it neatly and bake in a quick oven. To make sure it is quite cooked, get a clean piece of stick (of course a skewer is best if you have one), poke it through the middle of the pudding and if it comes out clean and with no pudding sticking to it—it should be ready to come out. Turn the pudding out on to a dish and sprinkle a little castor sugar over the top. Serve hot.

MacSymon's Stores,
LIMITED,

Canning Place,
LIVERPOOL.

Telegrams and Cables:
"EQUATOR, LIVERPOOL"

Telephone:
BANK 3753 (3 Lines)

European Stores
and
Camp Equipment

CHOP BOXES — FOR UP COUNTRY USE — A SPECIALITY.

Preserved Provisions, Groceries, Comestibles, Wines, Spirits, specially selected and packed for West Africa. MacSymon's are suppliers to the Crown Agents for the Colonies and Colonial Officials, Members of the West African Medical Force, and principal West African firms.

WRITE FOR EXPORT LIST

FINEST and LARGEST EXPORT PROVISION STORE
of its kind in the North of England.
All Goods delivered Free on board Steamer at Liverpool.

E. M. NUTTALL, Manager Export Department.

STEAMED DUFF.

This pudding is made exactly like the baked duff but do not turn it into a pie dish to bake it, instead of that, grease a pudding basin, put the mixture in it, tie your pudding cloth over the top as you do for a suet pudding, then place it in a saucepan of boiling water and let it cook for 1½ hours. It is good served with a white sweet sauce.

Don'ts—Don't let the water come over the top of the pudding. Don't let the water boil away. Don't forget to fill up again with boiling water. Don't forget to keep the lid well down on the saucepan all the time to keep the steam in. Don't forget to look inside every now and then to see that there is enough water in the pot.

DAINTY PUDDING.

Remarks—If made properly this is a very light pudding.

1 teacup of flour.
A pinch of salt.
1 tablespoon of sugar.
4 tablespoons of margarine or dripping or butter.
1 tablespoon of any kind of jam.
1 teaspoon of baking powder.
¼ teacup of milk and water.

Put into a basin the flour, salt, sugar, and rub in the fat. Mix all well together. Now add the jam. Put the milk and water in a small saucepan and make it just warm. Add the baking powder to the warm milk, and add these quickly to the flour, etc., stir well. Grease a pudding basin—put a very little jam at the bottom of the basin, pour in the mixture. Cover the basin with a clean piece of greased paper if you have it—if not, tie your pudding cloth over it. Put it in a saucepan of boiling water and let it steam for 4 hours.

Don'ts—Don't let the water come over the top of the basin it will quite spoil it if you do.

EGG JELLIES.

2 eggs.
1 tablespoon of lump sugar.
3 or 4 sheets of gelatine.
1 lime or lemon.
1 teacup of water.

Break the eggs into a basin and whisk them to a froth—whisk them for nearly ten minutes. Peel the lime or lemon very thinly—and squeeze the juice out. Put the peel, juice, sugar, gelatine, water and eggs into an enamel saucepan and stir over the fire for about ten minutes, taking care the egg does not curdle— so the fire must not be a very hot one. Pour it through a strainer into a basin and stir till it is nearly cold. Then wet one large mould or 3 or 4 small ones and pour the jelly in. When they are set, dip the mould into hot water for a second and turn out on to a glass dish. A little whipped cream served with this is very nice— if you have any.

FRITTERS.

½ breakfast cup of flour.
1 teacup of milk and water.
1 egg.
A little salt.
Sliced bananas or oranges.
3 tablespoons of dripping or lard.

Put the flour and salt in a basin, make a hole in the middle and drop in the yellow of the egg and the milk. Stir it gradually and make it into a batter. Whip the white of the egg to a stiff froth and add it lightly. Dip slices of the bananas or oranges in this batter. Have the dripping very hot in the saucepan—drop in the fritters and fry to a golden brown. Drain them on clean paper—sprinkle them with sugar and serve. Remember all batters are best when allowed to stand a little before they are cooked.

FRUIT TART.

1 tin or bottle of plums or cherries, or any fruit that cooks well.
1 breakfast cup of flour.
3 large tablespoons of dripping or butter.
3 teaspoons of sugar.
1 teaspoon of baking powder.
A pie dish.

Place an egg cup upside down in the middle of a pie dish. Half fill the dish with fruit-add the sugar—then fill up the dish with the best of the fruit and some juice. Put the flour into a clean basin—then see that your hands are clean. Take the dripping and rub it into the flour with the ends of your fingers, quickly and lightly till it all looks like breadcrumbs. Add the baking powder and mix round with a fork. Now add nearly a teacup of cold water and mix it well— if too stiff add a little more water—but add carefully, the paste must not be slimy but firm and come away clean from the basin.

Sprinkle flour on your pastry board and roller—and turn the pastry on to the board and sprinkle a little flour over that too. Then roll out quickly—always rolling away from you. Turn the pastry round and roll till it is about as thick as 2 water biscuits one on top of the other. It should be rolled till it is rather bigger than the top of the pie dish. Now cut off the rough edges about 1 inch wide. Dip a clean fowl feather into some water and wet round the edge of the pie dish—then place these strips of pastry round the edge of the dish—the rough edge nearest the fruit—the straight edge on the outside. With the feather, wet this strip of pastry all round and then take up your large piece of pastry and place it carefully right over the pie dish. Do not stretch it—but press the edge down lightly to the strip you have just made wet with the feather. Now hold up the dish in the left hand and with a sharp knife slice off any pastry that hangs untidily over the edge—cutting away from you with a quick sharp cut. Decorate the outside edge of the pastry with your fork (the handle end can be used, or mark in little lines with the back of the knife.)

Make air holes gently with a fork each side of the egg cup to let out the steam. Sprinkle the top with castor sugar, and bake in a nice hot oven for nearly ¾ hour.

Don'ts—Don't forget to have everything you want on the table before you begin. Don't forget to have clean hands. Don't make ornaments on the top of the pastry for a fruit tart—only on a meat pie. Don't put too much water into the flour at first, remember you can add more if you want it but you can't take it out when it is once in. Don't let the pastry be slimy—but soft and firm and dry—like dough for bread.

GOLDEN TOAST.

For the batter—3 tablespoons of flour, a pinch of salt, 1 egg, 1 teacup of milk (or milk and water.)
Some thin slices of bread.
Some jam.

Make the batter first and Let it stand for an hour. To make the batter—put the flour into a basin, make a hole in the middle and break an egg into it (find out first if the egg is a good one). Mix it smoothly—and add by degrees the milk. Beat the batter well with a wooden spoon and let it stand. Now cut. the bread into thin slices, take off the crust. It can be cut into neat rounds. Spread some jam on one piece and place another piece of bread on the top— making a jam sandwich. Do this with the other pieces of bread. Dip each piece or sandwich into the battier— have ready some boiling fat—a good deal—in a saucepan. Drop them in and fry till they are a nice brown. Turn them out on to a piece of clean paper and sprinkle them over with castor sugar and serve hot.

Don'ts—Don't cut the sandwiches much larger than a matchbox. Don't cover them too thick with batter, just dip them in to coat them.

BAKED JAM ROLL.

Ingredients: just the same as for open jam tart.

Flour your board and pastry roller, turn out the pastry, sprinkle flour on it and roll it out as if for a tart. Now spread some jam all over it but not too near the edges. Fold the piece nearest to you over and roll it till you get to the other end. Just wet the end lightly to make it stick and tuck the sides in carefully to keep the jam from coming out. Then put it on a floured baking dish and let it bake in a hot oven for about 15 or 20 minutes. It should look something the same shape as an omelette when finished. It must not be rolled tightly—more "folded" over. Can be served hot or cold.

LEMON SPONGE.

5 or 6 sheets of gelatine (½ oz.).
1 breakfast cup of water.
Rind and juice of a lemon or 2 limes.
1 tablespoon of sugar.
1 white of egg.

Melt the gelatine in the water, add the lemon rind (peeled very thinly) and sugar. Break the egg and put the white by itself into a basin. Strain the lemon juice on to it—then strain the melted gelatine on to that. Whisk all together till quite stiff so that the spoon could stand in it. Wet a mould and put it in— then turn out when quite cold on to a glass dish—or heap it all neatly on to a glass dish.

LAWN & ALDER Ltd.,

NAVAL, MILITARY & COLONIAL OUTFITTERS,

ESTABLISHED 1896.

22-24, KIRBY STREET, HATTON GARDEN, LONDON, E.C.1.

Cable Address: "UNPROVIDED, LONDON."
Codes: A.B.C. 5th & 6th EDITION.
Telephone: HOLBORN 1448-1449.

We cordially invite Visitors from overseas and all Travellers to visit our Showrooms when in town and inspect our Stocks of:—

CAMP EQUIPMENT, PROVISIONS, HOSIERY, BOOTS, HELMETS, TAILORING, GUNS, RIFLES, ETC.

SHIPPING INSURANCE & GENERAL AGENCY WORK IN ALL ITS BRANCHES.

MANGO FOOL.

6 or 8 good mangoes.
2 tablespoons of Ideal milk.
1 tablespoon of sifted sugar.

Take 6 or 8 good mangoes—peel them and take out the stone (or nut) with a knife. Put the fleshy part into a saucepan with a little water to cover them, and boil them till they are quite soft. Then put the hair sieve over a basin—pour the soft mangoes on the top of the sieve—then mash them through with the back of a wooden spoon. Now and then lift up the sieve and scrape the mashed mango off the inside—letting the pulp fall into the basin. When you have mashed through as much as you can, pour two tablespoons of Ideal milk into the basin and add the sugar. Stir all well together. Then when cool, pour into a glass dish. This is a good sweet, and served with dainty sweet biscuits or fingers of sweetened plain pastry, makes a good dinner sweet.

Don'ts—Don't pour too much water over the mangoes—the whole must be thick when finished like a thick soup.

MARMALADE PUDDING.

2 tablespoons of suet.
4 tablespoons of breadcrumbs.
3 tablespoons of flour.
2 tablespoons of sugar.
2 tablespoons of marmalade.
1 teaspoon of baking powder.
½ teacup of milk to mix.

Chop the suet very fine. Put it in a, basin, add the breadcrumbs, flour, sugar and baking powder. Add the marmalade and mix all together with the milk. Beat it well—it must not be too stiff, so if not enough milk, add more. Grease pudding basin, pour in the mixture. Tie a piece of greased paper over the top— or your clean pudding cloth. Place it in a saucepan of boiling water, put the lid on tight, and let it steam about 3 hours.

Don't—Don't let the water in the saucepan come over the pudding.

MOCK COFFEE MOULD.

2 breakfast cups of milk.
2 tablespoons of cornflour.
4 teaspoons of sugar.
1 tablespoon of treacle.

Put the cornflour into a basin and mix it to a paste with a little of the milk. Boil the milk and when it is rising in the pan, pour it over the cornflour and stir well. Return it to the saucepan, add the treacle and sugar. Stir till it is as thick as you want it. Then turn it into a basin—which must first be wetted, and when cold, turn out on to a cold dish. This sweet tastes very much as if flavoured with coffee essence.

OPEN JAM OR TREACLE TART.

1 small breakfast cup of flour.
2 tablespoons of dripping.
a pinch of salt.
1 small teaspoon of baking powder.
½ teacup of water.
A tin plate.

Put the flour into a basin, add the salt and baking powder—mix well and then rub in the dripping lightly with the ends of your fingers. Then add the water and mix well and quickly with a fork, if too stiff and dry add a little more water—but very carefully—do not slop in too much. Grease your tin plate (about as large as a pudding plate.) Now flour a board and rolling pin. Turn out the pastry—sprinkle a little flour over that and roll it out so that it is larger than the plate—but not too thin. Wet the edge of the plate with water. Cut strips of pastry and put them round the edge of the plate. Wet the edge again with a little water. Then take up the large piece of pastry that is left and place it right over the plate—and press gently the edges together. Hold up the plate, and with a knife, cut off the edges that are hanging over the plate. Decorate with your knife the edge of the pastry. Put some jam in the centre of the plate and with the pastry that is over, cut thin strips—give them a twist, and put them across the jam. Then bake in a nice hot oven for about 15 minutes. If you fill the centre with treacle or golden syrup or anything "runny", it is best to sprinkle fine breadcrumbs or biscuit crumbs on it— these keep it firm and prevents it running over the edge.

PANCAKES.

2 tablespoons of flour.
1 egg.
A teacup of milk and water (Ideal).
A pinch of salt.
1 large teaspoon or sugar.
A lime or lemon.
A little dripping or oil.
A small frying pan.

It is always better to make the batter about 1 hour before you want it and let it stand. Put the flour into a basin, break the egg into a teacup, and if it is good, make a hole in the flour and pour in the egg. Add gradually half the teacup of milk. Beat well with a wooden spoon and then add the rest of the milk. Now put a small frying pan on the fire—put in a teaspoon of oil or fat—let it melt and so grease the bottom of the frying pan. Now pour in enough batter to cover the bottom of the pan thinly. Lift it round the edges now and then with a knife, and when the under-part is a nice brown, jerk the frying pan up so that the pancake is tossed right over. A bold jerk is best and the pancake is then more likely to turn right over the first time. When it is cooked on the other side, turn it on to a piece of paper that is quite clean, shake a little sugar over it; roll it up quickly and put it on a hot dish to wait for the other pancakes, which make in the same way. Add a little more fat to the pan, and when quite hot, pour in some more batter and do exactly the same with this pancake as you did with the first. Toss it over when the under-part has browned. Cut a lime into four and serve round the dish.

Don'ts—Don't put the batter in the frying pan till the fat is quite hot. Don't put too much fat in the frying pan. Don't put too much batter—it just wants to cover the bottom of the pan thinly. Don't drop the pancake on the stove or the floor when you toss it; be sure to catch it again as it turns in the frying pan.

PINEAPPLE SWEET.

½ tinned or fresh pineapple.
1 breakfast cup of milk.
1 egg.
2 tablespoons of castor sugar.
1 small tablespoon of cornflour.

Cut the pineapple into small pieces—(other kind of fruit will do as well.) Lay them in a pie dish. Put the cornflour into a basin and mix it smooth with a little milk. Boil the rest of the milk and pour it on to the cornflour. Pour it back into the saucepan and let it cook for 2 or 3 minutes. Take it off the fire and add 1 spoonful of the sugar and the yolk of the egg. Pour this over the pineapple. Whip the white to a stiff froth—add the other spoonful of sugar. Pile on top of the custard and bake it crisp for about 15 minutes. If you have any angelica, decorate the top with a little.

PRINCESS PUDDING OR SOUFFLE.

Remarks—A pretty sweet for dinner but requires care and is some trouble to make well.

1 tin of apricots.
2 eggs (3 eggs if they are small.)
14 tablespoons of sugar.
1 teacup of milk.
4 oz. of gelatine (about 5 or 6 sheets.)

Stew the apricots and rub them through a hair sieve. Now separate the whites and yolks of the egg. Make the yolks and the milk into a custard. Add the sugar while the custard is hot. Melt the gelatine in 2 tablespoons of hot water and strain it into the custard. Pour this on to the apricot puree. (If you like, now add a few drops of cochineal to colour it, and some lemon juice.) Whip the whites of eggs to a very stiff froth, fold them carefully into the apricot when it is cool—then put into a mould.

PLAIN SWEET PASTRY FINGERS.
(To eat with Fruit.)

1 breakfast cup of flour.
2 tablespoons of butter or margarine.
1 teaspoon baking powder.
2 tablespoons of castor sugar.
½ teacup of water.

Put the flour into a basin—add the baking powder and sugar. Rub in the butter lightly till it all looks like crumbs. Mix it to a stiff paste with water—rather more than ½ a teacup may be required but add with caution. Flour a board and your rolling pin. Put the paste on it—roll out about as thin as a biscuit. Then cut into neat strips or rounds. Brush the top of each strip or round with a feather dipped in water—sprinkle on them a little castor sugar and bake in a quick oven for about 10 minutes.

GRACE BROTHERS
& CO. LTD.,
144, Leadenhall St. - London

MERCHANTS
IMPORTERS AND
EXPORTERS
FINANCIAL
SHIPPING AND
GENERAL
AGENTS

BRANCHES throughout United States, Canada, Argentine, Brazil, Chile, Peru, Bolivia, Ecuador, Colombia, Russia, Sweden, France, Italy, Spain, India, Ceylon, Japan, Australia, Africa (West and South), etc.

F. G. OSBORNE, Agent for Nigeria.

QUEEN OF PUDDINGS.

Remarks—This is a pretty pudding and suitable for a dinner sweet. Enough for 2 people.

1 teacup of breadcrumbs.
1 teacup of milk and water.
2 eggs.
2 teaspoons of sugar.
2 tablespoons of jam.
A small pie dish.

Put everything on the table that you will want. Grease the pie dish. Put the milk and water into a saucepan, and while it is heating, take the crusts off a stale piece of bread (about half a native made 3d. loaf), and crumble the bread into as fine breadcrumbs as possible. See that your hands are clean. Put the breadcrumbs into a basin with 1 teaspoon of sugar. Keep one eye on the milk so that it does not boil over— and as soon as it begins to rise in the saucepan take it off quickly and pour over the breadcrumbs. Now pour the breadcrumbs and milk into the pie dish.

Break one egg—put the yellow into a cup and the white into a basin. Break the other and divide it in the same way. Beat the yolks together with a fork for one minute, then stir them into the breadcrumbs and milk. put the pie dish in a hot oven for 20 minutes. While it is baking, whip the whites of the eggs to a stiff froth with the sugar, a good pinch of salt added to them will help to stiffen the froth. Whip slowly at first then quicker and always whip the same way—do not suddenly whip backwards. Now take the pudding out of the oven—spread the jam on the top and put the whipped egg and sugar on the top of the jam. It looks well put on roughly in little heaps—not smoothed over. Put the pudding back in a cool oven for about 10 minutes—when the top should be a pale brown and like "meringue." Serve at once.

Don'ts—The whites of the egg will not stiffen in five minutes, so don't stop whipping them for 10 or 15 minutes. Don't dump in the sugar in a lump—sprinkle it gently over the froth and then stir in quickly. Don't let the oven be too hot the second time you put the pudding in.

RICE MERINGUE.

1 teacup of rice.
2 breakfastcups of milk.
A little rind of lemon.
2 eggs.
A little sugar.
A tablespoon of jam.

Boil the rice in plenty of water for ¼ hour. Then strain. Put the rice into a saucepan with the milk, rind of lemon, and sugar. Boil all together till tender, then take out the rind. Separate the whites and yolks of eggs and beat the yolks well into the rice with a little butter. Put the mixture at the bottom of a pie dish, cover with a layer of jam. Beat the Whites of eggs with a little sifted sugar to a stiff froth. Spread over the jam and set in the oven till a light brown colour

SAUCER OR WAFER PUDDING.

2 tablespoons of flour.
4 tablespoons of butter.
2 eggs.
1 breakfast cup of (Ideal) milk and water.

Work the butter into the flour with the tips of the fingers—which must be clean. Beat the eggs together a second to mix them. Add them to the flour and mix. Add the milk and mix all together. Grease 5 or 6 saucers—not the best china ones. Pour a little mixture into each and bake them at once in the oven. Let the oven be nice and hot and bake them till they are brown—about an hour. Have ready on the table a clean sheet of paper. Sift some sugar on to the paper. Turn out the puddings on to the paper when they are done. Spread a little jam over each and fold over as you do an omelette. They must be served at once—hot.

STONE CREAM.

Remarks—This is a useful and simple sweet if milk is not scarce.

2 breakfast cups of milk.
4 tablespoons of sugar.
8 sheets (1 oz.) of gelatine.

Put the milk into a saucepan on the fire and when getting hot, add the gelatine and sugar. When these have melted, pour the whole into a mould and turn out when it is set and cold.

A more elaborate stone cream can be made by adding the following: — 1 tin apricots, some ground nuts.

Put the apricots in the bottom of a glass dish with a very little of the juice. Pour the cream over. When quite cold stick some ground nuts upright over the cream.

SWEET OMELETTE.

3 eggs.
½ tablespoon castor sugar.
1 tablespoon butter.
1 tablespoon jam.

Break the eggs carefully—putting the yellows into one basin, and the whites into another. Beat the yellows with the sugar till it is thick. Beat the whites to a stiff froth (a pinch of salt added to them helps wonderfully.) Then fold the white froth into the yellow mixture very lightly. Do not beat them together any more but just make the two mix by trying to "fold" the white into the yellow. Melt the butter and make it hot. Pour in the eggs and hold it over the fire for one minute. Then finish it in the oven— put the frying pan in the oven and let the omelette set. Then put the jam on the half nearest the handle of the pan—fold over the other half and serve very hot.

SUMMER PUDDING.

1 bottle of fruit.
Some bread.
4 tablespoon of sugar.

Blackcurrants, or redcurrants and raspberries are the best fruit for this pudding—but other fruits will do instead. Grease a small pudding basin— cut slices of bread rather thick, and line the basin with them. Stew the fruit without much water or juice but well sweetened. Pour the fruit into the middle of the basin. Place another slice of bread on the top, shaping it and making it fit as well as possible. Then place a saucer or plate on the top and a heavy weight on the saucer—so as to press the pudding well. When it is cold turn it out and cover it with custard or whipped cream.

TARTLETS.

Remarks—The pastry for these is made exactly like the pastry for the fruit tart—or open tart. But when the pastry is rolled out on the board, it is then cut with a round cutter, and put into patty pans to bake.

1 small breakfast cup of flour.
2 tablespoons of dripping.
A pinch of salt.
1 teaspoon of baking powder.
4 teacup of water.
6 or 8 tin patty pans.

Put the flour into a basin, add the salt and baking powder, mix them well with a fork. Then rub in the fat with the ends of your fingers lightly and quickly till it looks like breadcrumbs. Add the water and mix with the fork quickly—if it seems too dry and stiff, add just a little more water and mix. The dough should now be soft and smooth and come away clean from the basin. Sprinkle a little flour over the patty tins—or grease them if you like. Some people never grease their baking tins but just flour them. Sprinkle flour on your pastry board and roller. Turn out the pastry on to the board, sprinkle a little flour on that, then roll out quickly—always rolling away from you. Roll till it is about as thick as the edge of a pie dish. Now with a round pastry cutter, just a little larger than the patty pans, cut out as many rounds of pastry as you can. Cover the patty pans with them, decorate the edges if you like with the tip of the fork, and then place them in a hot oven—they should be done in about 10 minutes. Roll up the pastry again, sprinkle the board, rolling pin and pastry with a little flour once more, then roll out again and cut out more rounds. These cases of pastry will keep in a tin for two or three days and can be filled with jam or lemon cheesecake when required.

JAM TURNOVERS.

If you have no patty pans, then cut the rolled out pastry into small squares about the size of an ordinary envelope, place 4 teaspoon of jam in the centre, then wet the edges of the pastry and cross one corner over to the opposite corner and press the edges down all round.

SUET PUDDING—BOILED.

1 breakfast cup of flour.
½ breakfast cup of suet chopped fine.
1 teaspoon of baking powder.
A pinch of salt.
A large saucepan of boiling water.
A clean pudding cloth and some string.
A pudding basin.

Buy some fresh beef suet from the market. Shake a little flour over it—take the skin off and the stringy parts, and then chop it up very small. The flour keeps it from sticking to the knife in lumps. Put the breakfast cup of flour into a basin, add the salt, the baking powder and the chopped suet.

Odourless Sanitation
without Drains or Water-flush

ELSAN CHEMICAL SANITATION caters for every requirement in the safest, most effective and hygienic way.

Sewage is rendered immune from offensive odour and appearance. Bacteria is destroyed and continuous emptying of container avoided.

The New Elsan Catalogue gives some interesting information on this approved and Highly recommended system. May we send you a copy?

NEW ELSAN ECONOMICALLY PRICED SYSTEMS FOR RESIDENCES, CLUBS, FACTORIES, HOTELS, ETC.

ALSO NEW ASIATIC (SQUATTING PLATE) SYSTEM.

ELSAN MANUFACTURING Co.
51, Clapham Road, London S.W.9.

Agents for Nigeria.
JOHN HOLT & CO. Ltd.
P.O. Box 157, LAGOS.

Mix them all together with a fork. Add about ½ breakfast cup of water and mix all into a nice firm dough. If too dry, add just a little more water.

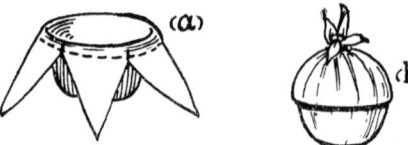

Grease a pudding basin and put the dough inside. Get a clean pudding cloth, hold the four corners together and dip the middle part into the saucepan of boiling water. Open it out on the table and sprinkle the middle part with a little flour. Tie this over the pudding basin, round the edge of the basin. Now bring the corners of the cloth up to the top and pin or tie together. Put an old saucer at the bottom of the saucepan to prevent the basin getting burnt, lower the basin into the water—put the lid on and let it boil hard for an hour or 1½ hours.

This is best served with golden syrup.

Don'ts—Don't begin to make the pudding till you have everything on the table you will want. Don't let the boiling water in the saucepan come over the cloth. Don't let the water boil away. Don't add cold water, add boiling water from a kettle.

SUET PUDDING—BAKED.

Remarks— This pudding is made exactly like the suet pudding boiled, but instead of putting it into boiling water, you bake it in the oven.

Grease a small pie dish. Put the dough inside it, and place in a hot oven for about an hour. Then turn it out on to a hot dish.

Don'ts—Don't forget to have a good hot oven. Don't let the oven cool till the pudding is done. Don't let the pudding burn, if the top is getting black, put a clean piece of paper over it.

A SIMPLE TRIFLE.

A sponge cake.
A breakfast cup of custard.
2 tablespoons of jam.
Some ground nuts.
2 table spoons of brandy, if liked, but not necessary.

If your cook can make a sponge cake this is a very simple and effective sweet for lunch or dinner. Make a sponge cake, but do not pour the mixture into a cake tin, pour it into a shallow and narrow baking tin. When it is cold cut it into about eight pieces. Arrange these on a glass dish. Then spread them with the jam, and, if you like, pour the brandy over them. Also sprinkle with chopped ground nuts. Then make a custard or make one with custard powder, and when neatly cool pour over the sponge cake. Split some ground nuts in half and stick them up straight all over the sweet.

WEST RIDING PUDDING.

The weight of 2 eggs in flour, fat and sugar.

The W. African egg usually weighs 1 oz. Therefore if you use 2 eggs you will require:

2 tablespoons of flour.
2 tablespoons of butter.
2 tablespoons of sifted sugar.
teaspoon of baking powder.
2 tablespoons of jam.
A few drops of vanilla, if you have any.

Cream the fat and the sugar, that is, put the sugar and fat together at the bottom of a basin and with a wooden spoon work them together round and round, and in time—about ten minutes—they should be smooth and white and like thick cream. Break the eggs into a cup, beat them together with a fork. Then add first a little egg, and mix. Then some flour, and mix. More egg, and then more flour, till you have used them all up. Then add the flavouring and the baking powder. Grease a pie dish. Spread the jam at the bottom. Put in the mixture, which should not quite fill the dish. Bake 1 hour to 1 hours in a moderate oven—not one that will burn it up quickly.

Don'ts—Don't let the jam burn. To prevent this place the pie dish on a baking tin.

SAVOURIES.

ANCHOVY TOAST.

4 or 6 anchovies.
1 hard boiled egg.
Cayenne pepper.
4 or 6 fingers of buttered toast.

    Dip the anchovies into boiling water, split them and take out the backbone (fillet them) and place them on the slices of buttered toast. Boil the egg for ten minutes till it is hard. Take off the shell and separate the white from the yellow. Chop up the white finely. Rub the yolk through a sieve and sprinkle some of each over the toast.
    If the yolk is rubbed through a wire sieve it comes out curly and light.

CAULIFLOWER AU GRATIN.

    Remarks. Cauliflowers are not easily grown in Nigeria, but as they make such a good savoury dish cooked in this manner, I have put in the recipe for those who are fortunate enough to procure one.

A cauliflower.
½ tablespoon of butter.
½ tablespoon of flour.
4 teacups of milk.
2 tablespoons of grated cheese.
A little cayenne pepper and salt.

    Pick off the outside old leaves, cut away the hardest part of the stalk and wash the cauliflower well in two or three changes of cold water to which some salt has been added. Have ready a pot of boiling water, put in the cauliflower and boil it with the lid off till the leaves and stalk seem quite tender—about 20 minutes to half-an-hour—but it depends on the size of the cauliflower. When it has boiled, strain off the water and press it with a clean cloth, or two spoons into a good shape. Drain all the water away thoroughly. Melt the butter in a stewpan, add the flour, mix smoothly, then add the milk. Bring it to the boil, stirring all the time—add the seasoning and half the cheese. Place the cauliflower neatly on a vegetable dish, pour this white cheese sauce over it, sprinkle the rest of the cheese on the top, and brown it in a quick oven. Serve very hot.

CURRIED EGGS ON TOAST.

4 eggs.
2 slices of crisp toast.
1 teacup of rich curried gravy.

Boil the eggs hard and chop them up. To make the gravy, see Spaghetti and Gravy, add one teaspoon of curry powder to that recipe for gravy. Have ready the toast, place the chopped eggs on it, then pour over it the curried gravy, and serve very hot.

CHEESE OMELETTE.

3 eggs.
1½ tablespoons of grated cheese (Parmesan).
1 tablespoon of butter.
A pinch of cayenne pepper and salt.

Break the eggs one by one into a basin. Do not put one on top of the other till you have seen if it is a good one. Beat them lightly, then add the salt and cayenne pepper. Melt the butter and let it get hot. Pour in the eggs and cheese and stir round. When the edges begin to set turn the omelette towards the. handle of the pan with your spoon and cook a nice brown. Serve very hot and at once.

CHEESE SAVOURY FOR TOAST.

1 tablespoon of butter.
4 tablespoons of Cheese (grated and heaped).
2 tablespoons of milk.
2 tablespoons or less of tomato chutney.
A medium sized onion.
A pinch of Cayenne pepper.

Melt the cheese in a saucepan, grate the onion. Prepare some buttered toast and keep it hot. Put the butter into a saucepan and add the onion. Cook for two minutes. Then add the milk, then the cheese, then the tomato chutney and cayenne and cook for another three minutes. Pour over the toast and serve very hot

CHEESE STRAWS.

2 tablespoons of flour.
4 tablespoons of grated cheese (Parmesan, if possible).
1 teaspoon of cold water.
1 tablespoon of butter.
The yolk of an egg.
A little cayenne pepper and salt.

Mix the flour, cayenne pepper and salt together. Rub in the butter with the tips of the fingers very lightly till all is like fine bread crumbs. Add the cheese, and mix with the yolk of egg and the water. It should now be a stiff paste. Flour a pastry board and your rolling pin—turn the paste on to the board—sprinkle a little flour on it and roll it out till it is about 1 inch thick. Now cut off the ragged ends, and cut into thin "straws" about the length of your finger, or if you like it better, cut into small rounds a little bigger than a penny. Bake on a greased tin in a not too hot oven for about ten minutes. Serve hot, or keep in a tin till they are wanted and crisp them up in the oven.

A dainty way to serve them is to put bunches of six or seven "straws" inside a ring of the pastry, or tie the bunches up with narrow ribbon and serve on a lace paper.

To make the ring of pastry cut out as many rounds as you want, then with a smaller cutter about two sizes smaller than the other one stamp out the middles, thus making a ring like a bracelet. Another way is to cut them in small rounds and serve as cheese biscuits.

Don'ts—Don't forget to have clean hands when you mix the paste. Don't put too much water into the flour, it must on no account be slimy, but quite stiff. Don't roll out too thin. Don't let them burn in the oven.

CHEESE PUDDING.

4 tablespoons of grated cheese.
1 teacup of milk and water.
2 teaspoons of flour.
1 egg.
Some pepper and salt.
½ teaspoon of baking powder (or a pinch of carbonate of soda).

Put the flour into a cup and make it smooth with a spoonful of the milk. Then put the rest of the milk into a saucepan. Grate or slice the cheese into it, then stir in the flour, pepper, salt, and baking powder (or carbonate of soda). Bring to the boil and when quite smooth pour all into a greased pie dish. Break an egg—the yolk into a cup and the white into a basin. Beat the yolk and add it to the pie-dish. Whip the white and stir that in gently. Put in a hot oven till it is brown and rises up. Must be served at once, very hot.

Don'ts—Don't make this long before it has to be served—twenty minutes should be long enough. Don't forget to have everything you want ready before you begin. The carbonate of soda is better than the baking powder if you can get it.

DEVILLED FOWL'S LEGS.

Legs of fowl or drumstick of turkey.
1 yolk of egg.
½ teaspoon of mustard.
Some salt and pepper.

Make two or three deep cuts in the meat. Mix the egg, salt, pepper, and mustard into a paste. Rub this into the cuts and over the meat. Toast or broil the legs over a clear fire or fry with a little fat in a saucepan.

BAKED EGGS.

4 eggs.
1 tablespoon of butter.
Some salt and pepper.

For this you want a shallow, fireproof dish. Butter the dish with half the butter. Then break the eggs carefully into the dish as you would poached eggs. Sprinkle a little salt and pepper them and put the rest of the butter in small pieces on the top. Place in a not too hot oven for about ten minutes till the whites are set. Serve very hot in dish in which they are cooked.

Telephone No. 57.   Telegrams: "AWOBOH, Lagos."

S. H. PEARSE

Head Office:

ELEPHANT HOUSE, LAGOS

EXPORT MERCHANT

Dealer in all kinds of
West African Produce

:: :: ORDERS SOLICITED :: ::

36 years' experience in West African Produce Trade.

Reference:

THE BANK OF BRITISH WEST AFRICA, LTD., LAGOS AND LONDON.

BUTTERED OR SCRAMBLED EGGS.

3 eggs.
1 tablespoon of butter (ground-nut oil does just as well).
A little pepper and salt.
1 tablespoon of milk.
2 rounds of toast.

Butter the toast and put it where it will keep hot. Break the eggs into a basin, add the milk, pepper, and salt, and beat lightly with a fork to mix them. Melt the butter in a saucepan, pour in the egg mixture and stir as quickly as you can with a wooden spoon till the eggs begin to set. Draw the saucepan away from the fire just a little, but let the mixture cook, and stir all the time. Then heap it up neatly on to the toast and serve hot. If you have any parsley chop up a little and sprinkle on the top.

Buttered eggs should look moist and very golden and shiny—never hard.

Don'ts—Don't forget that ground-nut oil does quite as well as butter and is cheaper.

EGG FRITTERS.

2 hard boiled eggs.
Some pepper.
3 or 4 drops of anchovy essence.
A little parsley, if possible.
½ teaspoon of anchovy paste.
2 tablespoons of bread crumbs.
1 raw egg.

Boil 2 eggs for ten minutes till they are hard. Shell and cut each egg in two. Take out the yolk and put it into a basin. Add to it the anchovy essence, and paste ad a pinch of pepper. Pound them together with the back of a wooden spoon. Then rub them through a (wire) sieve. Fill the whites of egg with this mixture. Break the other raw egg on to a plate. Mix it with a knife. Dip the halves of the eggs into the beaten egg, then cover with bread crumbs and fry them in hot fat. Serve very hot and garnish or decorate them with fried, chopped parsley.

POACHED EGGS.

3 eggs.
2 cups of water.
1 teaspoon of salt.
Some buttered toast.

Boil the water in a frying pan, add the salt. Break the eggs very carefully into the boiling water. Let it simmer for about two or three minutes till the whites begin to set, but the yolk should be soft. Take the eggs out carefully, one by one with a fish slice, drain away the water, trim the ragged edges of the white, and place on a piece of buttered toast. Or place them round a dish and pile well-fried bacon in the centre.

SAVOURY EGGS.

3 eggs, hard boiled.
1 tablespoon of butter.
tablespoon of anchovy sauce.
Some pepper.

Boil the eggs for about ten minutes, dip them into cold water and take the shells off fully. Cut them in half. Take out the yellow part and put in a basin. Add the anchovy sauce, pepper, and butter, and mix them well together. If you have a wire sieve rub the mixture through and it should come out the other side, all curly. Cut a little piece off the bottom of each case of white, so that it will stand up well on the toast. Now fill the white cases with the yellow mixture. Cut small rounds of bread, as large as a penny. Fry these, place them on a dish, and put an egg case on each. Or they can be dished on salad, or on a slice of tomato, but for a savoury at night the round of fried bread is best.

If you cannot get all the mixture back into the cases keep it well covered up and spread it on toast next day for a "gadget" or "small chop". If you have no anchovy sauce, chop up and use a little onion (and parsley), which will make them quite savoury.

KIDNEY OMELETTE.

3 eggs.
1 tablespoon of butter.
1 teaspoon of chopped onion.
Some pepper and salt.
2 tablespoons of chopped kidney.

Break the eggs one by one into a basin. Beat them lightly. Add the chopped onion, pepper, and salt. Put the butter into the frying pan. When it is quite hot fry the kidney in it for three minutes. Then pour in the egg and stir well. When it begins to set round the edges turn it over towards the handle of the pan with your spoon. Cook a few minutes longer, then turn it on to a hot dish and serve at once.

MACARONI CHEESE.

1 breakfast cup of macaroni.
½ tablespoon of butter.
A piece of cheese as large as a big mango.
1 breakfast cup of milk and water (Ideal).
A little salt and cayenne pepper.
½ teaspoon of made mustard.
½ tablespoon of flour.
2 saucepans (small).
1 pie dish.

Have some boiling water in one saucepan and throw into it the macaroni, broken up in lengths about the size of a match. Add a little salt. Let it boil till it is quite tender—about half an hour. Then put it on a sieve and throw away the water. Grate the cheese while the macaroni is boiling or shave it thinly with a knife, and put it on one side while you make the sauce. In the other saucepan melt the butter, stir in the flour with a wooden spoon, then add the milk—a little to begin with, then the rest. Stir all the time to prevent lumps. As it boils it should get thick. Then put in nearly all the grated cheese, some salt, cayenne pepper and the mustard, and the macaroni. Grease a small pie dish, turn the macaroni and the sauce into the dish. Sprinkle the rest of the grated cheese over it and brown it nicely in a hot oven.

Don'ts—-Don't put all the milk into the butter and flour at once. Don't put the cheese in in lumps. If you cannot grate it—then shave it thinly.

SAVOURY OMELETTE.

3 eggs.
1 tablespoon of butter or oil.
1 teaspoon of chopped parsley (if possible).
1 teaspoon of chopped onion.
1 tablespoon of chopped ham.
Some pepper and salt.

Break the eggs one by one into a cup. (That is break one egg into a cup—if good turn it into a larger basin—then try another egg the same way, then the third. By doing it this way you avoid mixing bad eggs (if you happen to have one) with the good. When the eggs are all in the basin, add the parsley and onion and ham, pepper and salt. Beat the eggs lightly, just to mix them. Have the butter quite hot in the frying pan, pour in the eggs, stir quickly to prevent the mixture sticking or burning. As soon as the edges are set fold it over towards the handle of the saucepan with your spoon (a wooden one). Cook lightly for a moment, then turn it on to a hot dish and serve. An omelette should not be quite set in the middle.

Don'ts—Don't beat the eggs to a froth. Don't turn the eggs into the saucepan till the butter, or oil, is quite hot.

SAVOURY ONIONS.

3 large onions.
A little salt.
White sauce.
2 tablespoons of grated cheese.
Some bread crumbs.
A pie dish.

Put 3 large onions into cold water and take off the outside skins. Put them into a saucepan of boiling water that covers them and add 1 teaspoon of salt. Cook till quite tender. Pour off the water and put the onions in a pie dish. Cover them with white sauce, flavoured with grated cheese. Sprinkle bread crumbs over them and place in a hot oven till they are brown. Serve very hot.

The Sauce.

½ tablespoon of flour.
1 tablespoon of butter or margarine.
¾ cup of milk and water (Ideal milk).
A little salt.
2 tablespoons of cheese.
A small, clean saucepan.
A wooden spoon.

Melt the butter in the saucepan. Stir in the flour quickly till it is well mixed. Pour in the milk, gently, stirring all the time, add the grated cheese and stir till it gets thick.

Don'ts—Don't pour in the milk too quickly—a little first and stir hard, then add the rest. There must not be any lumps in the sauce.

SAVOURY RICE—I.

Remarks—This is a light lunch dish and makes a pleasant change.

1 teacup of rice.
1 small onion.
3 tablespoons of grated cheese.
A little cayenne pepper.
Some salt.
1 teaspoon of butter.
A little chopped parsley, if you have any.
2 or 3 tomatoes.

Wash the rice in cold water first, then throw it into a saucepan of boiling water. Add the onion and let them boil for a quarter hour. If by this time you have too much water drain some away. When the rice is tender and nearly dry stir in the cheese, butter, cayenne pepper and salt—the tomatoes sliced up, and the parsley, if available. Let them all cook together for about ten minutes, and serve very hot.

Don'ts—Don't let the rice be too sloppy and wet, but it must not be as dry as you have it for curry. Don't forget to stir the rice when you add the cheese and the other things—it quickly sticks to the bottom of the saucepan.

SAVOURY RICE—II.

1 breakfast cup of rice.
1 tablespoon of grated cheese.
Some chopped parsley, salt and pepper.

Boil the rice till quite tender, and till most of the water is absorbed. Then add the grated cheese, parsley, salt and pepper. Serve very hot. Must be moist, but not sloppy.

TOMATO OMELETTE.

Instead of chopped kidney, tomato can be used for a change. Skin the tomato and cut it in small pieces and fry it a little before pouring the eggs into the pan.

TOMATO TOAST.

3 tomatoes.
4 rounds of buttered toast.
1 tablespoon of butter.
1 small onion.
1 egg.
1 tablespoon of browned bread crumbs.
A little pepper and salt.

Dip the tomatoes in boiling water, leave them in about two minutes, then the skin will peel off easily. Chop them up with the onion. Put the butter in a small saucepan and, when hot, fry the onion and tomato in this for five minutes. Add the egg, pepper and salt. Stir over the fire till thick. Spread on the toast. Sprinkle the browned bread crumbs over it and serve.

SAVOURY TOMATOES.

4 good sized tomatoes.
1 tablespoon of grated cheese.
4 small rolls of bacon.
1 tablespoon of butter.
4 tablespoons of bread crumbs.
A little pepper and salt.
4 rounds of buttered toast.

Cut the tops off the tomatoes and take out the insides carefully with the handle of a teaspoon. Put the bread crumbs, cheese, butter, salt and pepper into a basin and mix them together with the inside of the tomato. Place a little round of bacon (uncooked) on each, and then place all on a baking tin and bake in the oven for five or seven minutes. Serve them on buttered toast.

Co-operative Wholesale Society
LIMITED
30, Marina, Lagos, Nigeria

Head Office:
**Balloon St., Manchester
:: :: ENGLAND :: ::**

For all kinds of ..
High-class Provisions,
Drugs, Cottons and
.. Fancy Goods ..

Best Prices given for Produce.

Branches at Abeokuta and Kano.

WELSH RARE-BIT.

1 tablespoon of cheese.
1 tablespoon of butter.
1 teaspoon of made mustard.
1 egg (but not necessary).

Melt all these ingredients in a small stew- pan. Stir well with a wooden spoon. Have ready some hot, buttered toast. Pour the mixture over the toast. Serve at once—hot. This mixture must not be leathery or hard. Some cheeses will not cook well. Dutch cheeses are not very good for cooking purposes.

BREAD, CAKES ETC.

USEFUL HINTS FOR CAKE MAKING.

1. Small cakes or buns require a hotter and quicker oven than large cakes.
2. Do not open the oven door to look at them for 7 minutes for small cakes, 20 minutes for large ones.
3. Open and close the oven door gently—remember a bang or a knock will injure the cake and perhaps make it go flat.
4. Put a clean skewer, or a strong clean stalk of grass into the centre of the cake if you want to see if it is quite done—if it does not come out quite clean, bake the cake longer.
5. Don't move the cake in the oven till it has quite set.
6. Light sponge cakes and cakes with baking powder in them require a moderate oven.
7. Seed and pound cakes rather a hot oven.
8. A very light cake put into a very hot oven rises round the sides but is hollow in the middle.

Don'ts—Don't break eggs straight into flour, try them first one by one in a cup—for one bad one will spoil all the cake. Don't forget to have all the ingredients in front of you before you begin.

BREAD.

3½ breakfast cups of flour.
About ½ a yeast cake.
1 teaspoon of salt.
1 teaspoon of sugar (castor.)
1 breakfast cups of water—or 3 teacups.

Put the yeast and sugar into a basin and cream them together with a wooden spoon till they are liquid—that is—stir them together round and round. Add the water which must not be too cold. Put the flour into a large basin, make a well or hole in the centre, and strain the yeast and water into it. Work in a little flour from the sides, sprinkle the salt on the top, and put it in a warm place to rise. This is called "setting the sponge." When it has stood for 20 minutes, the top will be covered with bubbles. Now work all the flour in with your hand. When it is smooth, cover it up with a clean piece of old blanket or "house flannel," and set it to rise for 2 hours.

After that time take it up and knead it on a floured board for ¼ hour. Always work from the sides to the middle— knead with your fists as a washman pounds a cloth— doubling and turning it round and round. The dough should be smooth and springy—not sticky, more like a sponge. Divide the dough and make into smooth balls without any cracks. If the bread is baked in tins, flour them, put in the dough, and set them to rise for half an hour. Then put them in a very hot oven for a ¼ of an hour and then remove them to a cooler part for 4 hours. When done, stand the loaf on its side to cool.

Cooks will use native yeast for preference, but this gives the bread rather a sour taste, and if possible, it is better to bring out a few tins of yeast cakes, and have a fresh supply sent out every few months. If a piece of dough is kept back, it can be used for starting the next lot of bread—some people do not advise this except when using native yeast. Bread made with baking powder is better if formed into small rolls—not into loaves.

BREAKFAST ROLLS.

Remarks—These are very useful if you have run short of bread—They are quickly made.

1 breakfast cup of flour.
2 tablespoons of butter or margarine.
1 large teaspoon of baking powder and a little water.

Put the flour and baking powder into a basin—rub in the butter till it is all like bread crumbs. Then add the water—about ½ teacup to begin with, and stir with a fork.

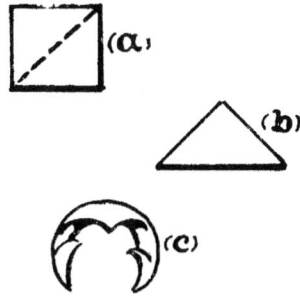

Flour a board, put the mixture on to it—cut it into four or five pieces. Roll each piece at a time as square as possible. Trim the edges. Cut each square across from corner to corner. Then roll a long edge towards the point and bend round like a horseshoe. An easier way is to take small pieces off the dough and place them on a baking dish in little balls. Brush them over with egg and bake 15 to 20 minutes in a hot oven.

CURRANT CAKE.

1 large breakfast cup of flour.
3 tablespoons of currants or sultanas.
3 tablespoons of castor sugar.
3 tablespoons of dripping.
1 egg.
¾ teacup of milk and water.
1 teaspoon of baking powder.
1 tablespoon of candied peel if possible.

Rub the currants with flour, clean them and pick out the stalks. Shave the candied peel very thinly and put both on one side. Put the flour into a basin and add the baking powder and ½ teaspoon of salt. Mix all well together. Now rub in the dripping lightly with the ends of your fingers which must be clean. Rub till there are no lumps of fat left. Now add the currants, candied peel and the sugar. Break the egg into a basin and add the milk to it—whisk them with a fork. Stir this to the flour and other ingredients, mixing all well together. Grease a cake tin (and line it with greased paper, if you like letting the paper come about 2 inches above the tin all round). Put the cake into a moderate oven and let it bake for one hour. After this take the cake out of the tin and stand it on a sieve, on its side, which will prevent it getting heavy.

Don'ts—Don't open the oven door for the first 20 minutes. Don't bang the oven door when you shut it again. Don't forget to put a skewer or thin piece of clean wood through the middle of the cake to see if it is done, before you finally take it out of the oven.

CHOCOLATE CAKE.

5 tablespoons of flour—sifted.
4 tablespoons of butter.
3 tablespoons of castor sugar.
3½ tablespoons of chocolate powder.
2 eggs.
½ teacup of milk.
1 teaspoon of baking powder

Cream the butter and sugar; that is, work them together in a basin till they become quite white—it takes a few minutes so do not give up too soon. Add the chocolate powder and the eggs (beaten) by degrees, mixing well all the time. Measure out the flour on to a plate or clean piece of paper, sift the baking powder into it, then stir it to the cake with the milk. First a little flour then a little milk and so on. Last of all add the vanilla. Bake in a very moderate oven, but a steady one for about one hour till the cake shrinks from the tin. The oven must not be a quick one and must not be allowed to cool off till the cake is done.

CHOCOLATE CAKES.

Remarks—These are not difficult to make, but require care.

3 tablespoons of butter.
2 tablespoons of sugar (castor).
1 tablespoon of grated chocolate.

2 tablespoons of flour (sifted).
2 eggs.

Cream the butter; that is, work it round and round in the basin with a wooden spoon till it goes white and looks creamy. Then break the eggs into a cup and beat them for a second. Now add the flour, and sugar, chocolate and eggs to the butter by degrees, a little of each at a time, mixing well. Beat the mixture well. Add now at the last a few drops of vanilla if you have it. Butter some little cake moulds. Half fill them with the mixture and bake for 15 minutes. They can be baked in patty pans and make a nice change for afternoon tea.

GINGER CAKE.

1 breakfast cup of flour.
2 tablespoons of sugar.
1 tablespoon of ground ginger.
2 teaspoons of baking powder.
2 eggs.
2 large tablespoons of dripping or margarine.
½ a breakfast cup of black treacle.
½ a teacup of milk and water.

Grease the cake tin. Cream the fat and sugar. That is, put them together into a basin and work them round and round with a wooden spoon till they "cream" and go nearly white. This may take 5 to 10 minutes. Then break the eggs into a cup and beat them a second with a fork. Weigh out your flour on to a piece of paper or plate and put the ginger and baking powder on to it and mix them lightly. Now pour first a little egg on to the sugar and fat and mix, then a little of the flour and mix, then more egg, and so on till the egg and flour are well mixed in. Now beat in the treacle and the milk and when all is well mixed, pour it into the cake tin, and bake in a not very hot oven for at least one hour; it may want to be in longer. Try the middle with a skewer. When it is done turn on to a sieve to cool, or place it on the bottom of the cake tin, which should stand in water to keep the ants away.

Don'ts—Don't put in the egg and flour till the sugar and butter are quite creamy. Don't use a metal spoon if you have a clean wooden one.

If this mixture is put on a narrow, small baking tin it makes a good ginger slab. Some split ground nuts placed on the top of the ginger cake before baking it gives it a nice appearance. This mixture put into a pudding basin and steamed is very good.

GINGER SLAB.

10 tablespoons of flour (heaped).
3 tablespoons of sugar (level).
3 tablespoons of fat (heaped) margarine or dripping.
2 teaspoons of ground ginger.
½ teaspoon of salt.
½ teaspoon of carbonate of soda.
3 tablespoons of treacle (heaped).
1½ teacups of milk.

Have everything you will want on the table before you begin. A shallow tin, the kind used for baking, or for Yorkshire pudding is best. Then in a large clean basin mix all the dry ingredients, the flour, sugar, ground ginger, salt. Then rub in the fat—next the treacle (Fowler's West Indian is the best). Just warm the milk and mix the carbonate of soda with it. Beat it into the mixture gradually. Beat well. Bake in a slow oven in a Yorkshire pudding tin.

Don'ts—Any cake or pudding with treacle in it burns very easily, so don't have an oven as hot as you would for pastry; let the heat be moderate all the time.

MILK CAKES.

2 breakfastcups of flour.
1 breakfastcup of milk.
2 tablespoons of butter or margarine.
1 dessertspoon of baking powder.

Mix the flour and baking powder, rub in the butter and mix lightly with the milk. Flour board, roll out very lightly and not too thin. Divide into 12 cakes and bake for 20 minutes.

ROCK BUNS.

1 breakfast cup of flour.
2 tablespoons of cleaned currants (or sultanas.)
3 tablespoons of sugar.
1 teaspoon of baking powder.
½ tablespoon of candied peel (if you have any)
1 salt spoon of grated nutmeg.
2½ tablespoons of dripping or margarine.
2 eggs.
¼ teacup of milk and water.

Have everything ready measured before you begin. Put the flour and baking and sugar into a basin and rub in the dripping till there are no lumps and it looks like breadcrumbs. Clean the currants (and if you have candied peel, shave it very thinly with a sharp knife.) Add the currants, candied peel and nutmeg. Mix all these dry ingredients together. Beat the eggs in a cup for a second, add the milk to them and pour them on to the flour, etc. Mix all well together. With a fork take up some mixture and drop it on to a floured baking tin. A lump about the size of a kola nut is large enough as the mixture spreads when baked. Bake in a quick oven for about ¼ of an hour. The buns should look rough and knobbly when finished.

CURRANT CAKE.

This mixture can be put into a floured cake tin and baked for about 1 hour. Try the middle with a skewer. Then turn on to a sieve to cool.

SANDWICH CAKE.

Remarks—Two round tins about the size of a cheese plate with the edge turned up all round are required for this cake, so that it is not an easy one to make in this country unless you have these tins. The mixture rises so the edge of the tin must be turned up to prevent it over-flowing. But if the difficulty of a proper tin can be overcome, the cake is useful for tea or a dinner sweet.

2 tablespoons of butter.
4 tablespoons of sugar.
6 tablespoons of flour.
1 egg, or 2 if they are small.
¾ teacup of milk.
1 teaspoon of baking powder or, if you have it
¾ teaspoon of cream of tartar and ¼ teaspoon of carbonate of soda.

Cream the butter and half the sugar—i.e., put both into a basin and work them round together with a wooden spoon till they are creamy and thick, this takes about 7 to 10 minutes. Then add the rest of the sugar and work that in. Break the egg into a cup and beat it with a fork. Add the milk to the egg and mix them with the fork. Have the flour measured out on a plate or clean piece of paper and add the baking powder to it. Then to the creamed butter and sugar add first some flour and then some egg and milk mixing well the whole time.

Grease and dust with flour two sandwich tins, divide the mixture and spread it evenly and bake in a quick oven 8 to 10 minutes. Turn them out on to clean paper that has been sifted with a little sugar and put jam on one half and the other half on the top. Any other filling can be used—lemon curd, chocolate icing—or butter cream—this latter is very good.

BUTTER CREAM.

2 tablespoons of butter.
4 tablespoons of icing sugar.
1 tablespoon of water or flavouring.

Cream the butter, i.e., work it round with a spoon till it goes creamy—put in the sugar and water and mix it till it looks thick and smooth like butter Add more water if necessary.

SCONES

1 breakfast cup of flour.
1 good teaspoon of baking powder.
1½ tablespoons of butter or margarine.
½ tablespoon of castor sugar.
1 teacup of milk and water.

Sift the flour into a basin with the baking powder. Rub in the butter lightly with the ends of the fingers till it looks like crumbs—mix in the sugar. Add the milk and water and mix quickly. Sprinkle a board with flour—put the mixture on to the board. Roll it out—but not too thin—cut into rounds and bake for 25 minutes. When they are done brush them with a little milk. These can be split in two and buttered. They are nicest eaten hot.

If you can possibly make them with 1 teaspoon of cream of tartar, teaspoon of carbonate of soda instead of baking powder, they are lighter and better.

SPONGE CAKE

Remarks—This is a most economical cake and very simple to make if the cook only has patience to beat the eggs long enough.

3 eggs.
3 level tablespoons of castor sugar.
2 heaped tablespoons of flour.
A small cake tin about 5 inches across
A good egg whisk.

First of all grease your cake tin very well and while the grease is still soft, mix a teaspoon of flour and a teaspoon of sugar together.

Throw this into the cake tin and shake it all over it till it is nicely coated. Take the tin with one hand, tap it gently with the other, turning the tin round on its edge at the same time so that the sides get well coated too. This will form the nice crust—like shop sponge cakes have—when baked. If you have a sifter—now sift the flour on a plate or piece of paper. Then break the eggs one by one into a cup. If they are good, pour them into your mixing basin. If the 1st egg is good pour that into the basin, then try the second, and if good, add it to the first—then try the third.

Put the 3 tablespoons of sugar on to the eggs and beat these together for at least ¼ of an hour. Always beat the same way—if one arm aches, change the whisk to the other hand but beat the same way. This is very important. There is no need to beat at a great pace. The egg and sugar should be nice and thick and nearly white and full of bubbles by the end of a ¼ of an hour. Sprinkle the flour in lightly and mix it—fold it in with the whisk—but do not beat it any more. Now pour it quickly into the cake tin and put it at once into a nice hot oven—but not a fierce one. When the cake shrinks away from the tin and looks dry and firm on the top it is done. About half an hour is the usual time. Turn it out on to a sieve and let it steam for a little.

Don'ts—Don't open the oven door for 20 minutes— if the top seems to be burning place a piece of paper over it. Don't bang the oven door or the cake will go flat. Don't leave the cake where the ants can get to it. When it is cool it is best to place the cake tin upside down in a plate of water—put the cake on the tin and let it stay there for a while. Don't stop beating the cake when once you have begun. Don't begin therefore till you have round you all you will want—the flour measured out—the cake tin greased. Don't beat less than ¼ hour. Don't put the eggs on top of each other till you have seen if each one is good.

If you chop up small a handful of nuts and sprinkle them in the mixture as you pour it into the cake tin, it varies the cake and is very good.

FORTNUM & MASON

have long made a special study of the requirements of European Residents in Tropical Africa. The conditions and needs of life at Headquarters and in the Bush are understood and appreciated. Every possible variety of Provisions and Equipment is supplied and correctly packed to suit Native Transport and to withstand the roughest handling.

¶ Special arrangements have been made for the convenience of Government Officials, and enquiries in this connection are respectfully invited.

FORTNUM & MASON
:: :: 182, Piccadilly :: Ltd.
LONDON   **ENGLAND**

Cables:
"FORTNUM
LONDON"

Codes:
A.B.C.(5th Edition)
Bentley's

'SQUASHED FLY' BISCUITS.

1 breakfast cup of flour.
2 tablespoons of sugar.
2 large tablespoons of dripping or butter.
2 tablespoons of cleaned currants.
1 teaspoon of baking powder.
1 egg.
½ teacup or more of milk and water.

Have all the ingredients measured out on the table in front of you—then you are not likely to forget any. Clean the currants first by rubbing them in flour and picking out the stalks, etc. Now mix all the dry ingredients together. Put the flour into a basin and add the sugar and baking powder and rub in the dripping or butter with the tips of your fingers till there are no lumps. Add the currents and mix. Break the egg into a cup, if it is good add the milk and water to it and beat them for a second with a fork. Add them to the flour, etc., and mix well. If too dry add a little more milk and water or another egg. You want the mixture like pastry. Sprinkle flour on to a board, put the pastry on to it, sprinkle that with a little flour, also your rolling pin (or glass bottle), and roll out the pastry rather thin. Then cut it into rounds with the lid of a tin if you have no cutter—or into squares or fingers with a knife. Flour a baking tin—place the biscuits on it. and bake in a hot oven for about 20 minutes or more.

Don'ts—Don't put in too much milk and water— the pastry must not be too! wet or sticky, but firm and springy. Don't let the pastry stick to the Board, or rolling pin—a little flour sprinkled on either will prevent this. Don't forget to have a hot oven.

WAFER BISCUITS.

1 breakfast cup of flour.
2 tablespoons of butter.
½ teaspoon of salt.
Some milk.

Put the flour into a basin and rub the butter into it lightly and well with the ends of the fingers. Mix into a stiff paste with the milk. If 1½ tablespoons is not enough add a little more carefully. Sprinkle a board with flour and put the paste on to it and beat it all over for quite ten minutes to make the biscuits full of bubbles. Roll out as thin as possible— but do not work in any more flour than is necessary to prevent the paste sticking to the board. Cut into large square biscuits and bake in a quick oven to a very pal's brown.

WATER BISCUITS.

1 teacup of flour.
1 tablespoon of butter.
A pinch of salt.
Some cold water.

Put the flour into a basin and rub the butter into it lightly with the ends of your fingers. Add the salt and mix with enough cold water to form a stiff sticky paste. Try two tablespoons of water first, if not enough add a little more, cautiously. Flour a board lightly—turn out the paste and beat well with a rolling pin. Roll out very thin and cut into rounds. Place them on a baking tin and prick them all over with a fork. Bake for a few minutes in a quick oven till they are a pale brown.

PROVISIONS

Place your Orders with the oldest and most reliable Provision Merchants in the Colony

PICKERING
and
BERTHOUD
—LIMITED—

Tel. Address:
PICKERING,
LAGOS.

LAGOS.

Telephone No. 55.

We specialise for European Trade . and Up-Country Residents .

Our large and varied stock combined with prompt delivery ... will ensure satisfaction ...

GENERAL · OUTFITTERS

SAUCES.

GENERAL RULES FOR MAKING SAUCES.

For a pouring sauce use 1 tablespoon of fat, 1 tablespoon of flour to 2 breakfast cups of liquid.

For a coating sauce use 2 tablespoons of fat, 2 tablespoons of flour to 2 breakfast cups of liquid.

BROWN SAUCE.

1 small onion.
1 tablespoon of dripping.
1 tablespoon of flour.
2 breakfast cups of water or stock.
A little salt.

Skin and slice the onion. Melt the dripping in a saucepan. Fry the flour and onion until brown (do not burn it). Add half a cup of the liquid. Stir well. Then add carefully the rest of the liquid. Put in the salt, bring to the boil and then let it cook quietly for 15 minutes. This sauce may be strained if desired.

The flavour may be improved by adding 1 teaspoon of Worcester sauce or other relish.

BROWN GLAZE FOR BEEF ROLL

1 teacup of clear stock.
1 tablespoon of gelatine or 4 or 6 sheets.
½ teaspoon of Bovril or browning.

Put all these into a saucepan on the side of the fire and let them get hot, till the gelatine has melted. If the gelatine is in sheets tear it into pieces. Do not stir the mixture as that makes the glaze look muddy. Do not boil it as that will make it like glue—just let it melt slowly, Now let it cool in the saucepan. Then pour some of it gently over the roll, dabbing it with a clean feather till the roll is well covered. Let the first layer set firm, then pour on another. And if it does not look well covered pour on a third layer.

MAYONNAISE SAUCE FOR SALADS—1.

2 yolks of eggs.
¼ teacup of salad oil.
1 small tablespoon of vinegar.
1 small tablespoon of Tarragon vinegar.
1 teaspoon of made mustard.
Some salt and pepper.
1 small tablespoon of boiling water.

Break the eggs carefully and put the yolks into a basin. Add the salt, pepper and mustard, and stir. Then pour the oil in most carefully, drop by drop, always stirring. It should set very thick. Then pour in the vinegar gradually. Add the boiling water. This sauce, if bottled, will keep good a long time.

MAYONNAISE SAUCE—2.

1 yolk of egg.
1 teaspoon of castor Sugar.
1 teaspoon of made mustard.
A little pepper and salt.
2 small tablespoons of oil.
2 small tablespoons of vinegar.
1 breakfast cup of cream.
1 tablespoon of boiling water.

Mix the yolk of egg, sugar, mustard, pepper, and salt together. Then add the oil, drop by drop. Then the vinegar, very slowly. Then the cream or Ideal milk. Then the boiling water, which should keep the whole from curdling. Mix hard the whole time.

ONION SAUCE.

2 onions.
1 teacup of milk and water.
1 tablespoon of flour.
1 large teaspoon of butter, some pepper and salt,
A small saucepan.

Peel the onions, cut them into four and boil them in a little water till they are tender. Now drain the water off and throw it away and put the onions on a plate till they are wanted. Put the butter in the saucepan, and when it is melted, stir in the flour. Then add the milk, a little at first, then the rest. Then add the onions, chopped up, but not too small, also the salt and pepper. Stir all the time till the sauce begins to get thick, then draw it away from the fire, if you do not want it to get any thicker.

Don'ts—Don't let there be any lumps in the sauce. To avoid this put a little milk in at first and stir it with the flour till it is smooth. Then add the rest gradually.

WHITE SAUCE.

1 tablespoon of butter or dripping.
1 tablespoon of flour.
2 breakfast cups of milk, or milk and water.
A little pepper and salt.

Melt the butter in a saucepan; draw the pan to the side of the fire. Add the flour and mix well with the back of a wooden spoon. Add half a cup of the liquid and stir carefully till boiling. Add the rest of the liquid gradually, bring to the boil and boil for three minutes, stirring well all the time. Add the salt and pepper.

This is the foundation for many sauces, as for example——

SWEET SAUCE.

Add to the White Sauce 1 small tablespoon of sugar and, of course, leave out the salt and pepper.

PARSLEY SAUCE.

Add to the White Sauce 1 small tablespoon of finely chopped parsley.

CAPER SAUCE.

Add to the White Sauce 1 small tablespoon of chopped capers and 1 small tablespoon of caper vinegar.

CHEESE SAUCE.

This may be served with boiled cauliflower or other vegetables. Add to the White Sauce 2 tablespoons of grated cheese.

FISH SAUCE.

Use fish stock instead of milk and add anchovy essence or shrimps.

SICK ROOM

THIN BARLEY WATER.

2 tablespoons of pearl barley.
The rind of a lemon.
2 lumps of loaf sugar.

Wash the barley and put it into a jug; peel a lemon very thinly and put it with the sugar into the jug with the barley; then pour 2 breakfast cups of boiling water into it, cover it up, and let it stand till cool, then strain it through a piece of clean muslin or a very clean strainer.

THICK BARLEY WATER.

2 tablespoons of pearl barley.
4 breakfast cups of water.
Rind of a lemon.
4 lumps of sugar.

Wash the barley well in several waters, boil it for two hours in 4 breakfast cups of water. Peel a lemon very thinly, and put the peel into a jug. When the barley water has boiled for two hours strain it into the jug on to the lemon peel. When it is cool take out the lemon peel and sweeten it to taste with about 4 lumps of sugar. Two small limes might be used if is not possible to get a lemon.

BARLEY MILK.

2 breakfast cups of milk.
½ breakfast cup of "patent" barley.

1 breakfast cup of water.
Sugar to taste.

Boil the barley in the milk and water for two hours, sweeten it with a little sugar, and serve it while it is just warm.

BARLEY WATER MADE WITH PATENT BARLEY.

1 tablespoon of patent barley.
4 breakfast cups of water.
Rind of 1 lemon or 2 limes.
Loaf sugar.

Mix 1 tablespoon of patent barley to a smooth paste with about a wineglass of cold water, then pour 4 breakfast cups of boiling water on to this, and stir while boiling for five minutes. Put the lemon peel into a jug, pour the barley water on to the peel. When cold remove the peel and sweeten with loaf sugar to taste.

BEEF TEA.

A good piece of fresh lean beef.
1 breakfast cup of cold water.

Take the beef and cut it up very finely, taking away all the skin and fat, then put the meat into a stone jar or a clean native pot with one breakfast cup of cold water. Put the lid on the jar or pot and tie a piece of paper over it. Stand the jar in a saucepan of boiling water for three hours or in the oven for 1½ hours. After that time pour the beef tea into a warm cup. Salt according to taste.

Beef tea must not boil.

CUP OF ARROWROOT.

1 small tablespoon of arrowroot.
1 breakfast cup of milk.

Put the milk in a clean pan on the fire to boil. Put the arrowroot into a basin, add to it by degrees a little cold milk and stir it into a smooth paste. When the milk in the pan is quite boiling pour it on to the mixed arrowroot and stir well with a wooden spoon to make it smooth: serve with sugar or salt.

Bermuda arrowroot is the best, but very much more expensive than other kinds.

GRUEL WITH PATENT GROATS.

2 small tablespoons of patent groats.
2 breakfast cups of water or milk.

Put two spoons of groats into a basin, and mix to a smooth paste with a little cold milk or water. Put the rest of the milk or water into a pan on the fire to boil. When it is boiling pour it on to the groats stirring well with a wooden spoon, then pour it back into the pan and let it boil for ten minutes. Take care that it is not lumpy, and serve with sugar or salt according to taste. If it seems too thick boil a little more milk or water and stir it in.

LEMONADE.

2 lemons or limes.
Loaf sugar.

Put a kettle of water on the fire to boil. Peel very thinly the lemons and cut off all the white pith, then cut them into thin slices and take out all the pips; put half the rind and the slices of lemon into a jug, then add loaf sugar to taste. When the water is quite boiling, pour 2 breakfast cupfuls into a jug, cover it over and leave it to cool, and when cold strain it into another jug through a piece of clean muslin.

SAVOURY CUSTARD.

Break the yolks of 3 eggs and the white of one into a basin, add the stock and some salt, and whisk well together; pour the mixture into a greased gallipot cover it with a piece of buttered paper, tie it down, put it into a saucepan of boiling water; and let simmer k for a quarter of an hour; after that time take the gallipot out and the custard on a plate to cool.

OXO.

Oxo can be made with milk instead of water. It forms a nourishing food, but is not very palatable.

ODDS and ENDS.

SERVICEABLE MEASURES.

1 breakfastcupful is equal to ½ lb. flour.
1 teacupful is equal to ¼ lb. flour.
1 tablespoonful is equal to 1 oz. of dry substance.
1 dessertspoonful is equal to 1 oz butter or dripping.
1 teacupful is equal to 1 gill.
1 tumblerful (table) is equal to ½ pint.
½ cupful of milk for moistening ½ lb of flour.
A teaspoon holds a drachm.
A tablespoon holds ½ oz.
A teacup holds 5 ozs.
1 pint is equivalent to 1 lb.
1 oz. of butter is 2 level teaspoons.
1 oz. of sugar is 2 level tablespoons.
1 oz. of flour is 4 level tablespoons.
1 oz. of cornflour is 3 level tablespoons.
1 oz. of ground coffee is 5 level tablespoons.
I oz. of cocoa is 3 level tablespoons.
1 oz. of pepper is 4 level tablespoons.
1 oz. of mustard is 4 level tablespoons.
1 oz. of chopped suet is ¼ of a cupful.
1 oz. of olive oil is 2 tablespoons.

These measures are, of course, very rough, but a great help when cooking.

TO TAKE STAINS OFF CUPS AND TEAPOTS.

Rub the stain with damp salt, and it should disappear very quickly.

TO CLEAN GREASY PLATES OR KNIVES, ETC.

It is a good plan to wipe the grease off first with pieces of paper, which must be collected and burnt directly afterwards. This way saves the washing basin and cloth from getting full of grease.

IRONMOULDS.

To remove iron moulds or stains from linen or any wearing apparel, a tube of "Movol", which can be bought at any chemists or grocers, is invaluable. It is a great success.

LUX.

To get the best results from Lux I find it is best to put about a tablespoonful into a clean, dry basin, then pour boiling water from a kettle on to it; it immediately melts and makes good suds. Cold water can then be added till it is as cool as you want it. Woollen jerseys and blankets can then be squeezed and dipped in this without fear of them shrinking.

TO REMOVE INK STAINS FROM LINEN.

Cut a lemon and squeeze the juice on the stain. Then rub with yellow soap and rinse in cold water. This is effectual if done at once; will not remove an old stain.

Candle-grease spots can be removed by placing a piece of blotting-paper over the spot and holding a hot iron over it.

Carbonate of soda will generally remove the most obstinate mud stains. Rub with cloth or flannel, then press well with an iron on the wrong side.

TO ABSORB DAMP IN A CUPBOARD.

Fill a small box with lime and place on a shelf. This will result in the air of the cupboard being kept dry and sweet.

LAMP CLEANING.

Cut lamp wicks very occasionally. Instead of cutting, rub the burnt part with a piece of soft paper or rag. If you can get your boy to use soft newspaper or old advertisement catalogues to clean the lamps and chimneys with, it does away with old oily rags and prevents good dusters or pantry cloths being used. If a piece of paper is wrapped round the chimney cleaner and worked gently up and down, inside the chimney and outside, it removes all stains and gives the glass a sparkle. The paper can also be used to remove all the oil from the outside of the lamp. The paper can then be all thrown away each day, and no oily rags left lying about. An old toothbrush is a good thing with which to brush off all charred wick and dust from the network inside that crosses the lamp near the wick.

The lamps should be cleaned every day, and the wicks turned down till the evening. Glass chimneys should not be washed; cleaned with paper and rubbed with a soft cloth is all they want.

SOAP.

If household soap bought by the bar is cut up in nice chunky pieces and arranged on the storeroom shelf to dry, with a little space between each piece, it will keep much longer and not waste so when used.

HOMEMADE DRIPPING.

Your cook can buy about 6d. worth of fat in the market. Let him cut it up and put it into an iron saucepan with enough cold water to cover it. Boil it quickly, without the lid on, stirring it every now and then till the water has all boiled away and the fat begins to get crisp and brown. When a little cool, strain it into a jar or glass with a screw top and it is ready for use.

Don'ts—Don't pour it boiling hot into the jar or glass, it will crack them.

TO CLARIFY FAT.

Pour it out of the dripping-pan, while it is hot, into a basin with about a glassful of cold water; when it is cold, take the cake of dripping off the water, scrape all the "bits" off the bottom of the cake and wipe it dry. Throw away the water which will not be clean.

FAT FOR FRYING.

Ground nut oil is generally used, but the home-made dripping is excellent for this. Strain it while it is hot every time it is used, and if it gets very brown, strain it into a basin of cold water. The clean fat will rise to the top, the "bits" all fall to the bottom. It can be used over and over again and should keep quite fresh.

Don'ts—Don't use the fat in which you have fried fish for anything else. Keep it separate and use it only for fish.

Ground nut oil can be used instead of butter or margarine for buttered eggs, and does perfectly well. Also for salad dressing instead of olive oil. It can also be used for greasing pie dishes, cake tins, arid patty pans, etc.

TO MAKE BROWNING FOR GRAVIES AND SOUPS.

1 breakfastcup of sugar (lump or brown).
1 breakfastcup of water.

Choose an old saucepan. Put the sugar into it and cook it gently till it turns a deep coffee colour. Put in the water by degrees. When the sugar is all melted, let it cool, then strain it into a bottle.

Only a few drops of this is needed to colour gravy, so it should last three or four months.

Don'ts—Don't put in the water all at once because the hot sugar fizzles and "spits" and throws off much steam when the cold water touches it, so put the water in very gradually.

TO SKIN TOMATOES.

Put some boiling water into a pudding basin, dip the tomatoes in, leave them for one or two minutes. Take them out, and you will find the skin comes off them very easily.

PICKLE FOR MEAT—1.

2 breakfast cups of salt.
6 tablespoons of brown sugar.
1 tablespoon of saltpetre.
1 gallon of water, or
16 breakfast cups of water.

Put all these ingredients into a large saucepan and let them boil for five minutes. Skim any dirt off the top of the water, then strain it into 'a large basin, and when it is cold the meat can be put in it and should be kept in it five days.

Turn the meat over each day, and look at it to see if it is keeping good.

PICKLE FOR MEAT—2.

4 breakfastcups of salt.
4 tablespoons of saltpetre.
1 tablespoon of brown sugar.
2 gallons of water.

Boil all these together for 5 minutes, skimming well. Strain it into an earthenware pan. The meat can be put in as soon as the mixture is quite cold, and should remain in it 5 or 6 days.

SALT BEEF.

Rub the beef well all over with salt and sprinkle a teaspoonful each of brown sugar and powered saltpetre over the meat.
2nd day—Rub well with salt.
3rd day—To be well rubbed with the brine.
4th day—Ready to cook.
Put into very little cold water—bring quickly to a boil. Have ready a carrot, onion, turnip, a sprig of parsley and 2 cloves and 3 or 4 peppercorns. When it comes to the boil after the vegetables are added, draw back and simmer very slowly. 20 minutes to each lb. Allow the meat to cool a little in the water—then press between two dishes with a weight on the top.

HOME-MADE BAKING POWDER.

Remarks—This is, of course, far cheaper to make than to buy in tins if the difficulty of getting tartaric acid can be overcome.

4 tablespoons of cornflour.
4 tablespoons of carbonate of soda.
3 tablespoons of tartaric acid.

Mix all these together, then pass them through a sieve twice, and put into air-tight tins or bottles.

ORANGE MARMALADE.

Remarks—This recipe is for bitter oranges; if sweet oranges are used less sugar would be required, and perhaps some limes or lemon added if liked.

2 lbs. of oranges.
3 lbs. of sugar.
The rule is, to every lb. of oranges put 1½ lbs. of sugar.

Put the oranges whole into a large pan and cover them with cold water; then boil them till they are quite soft. When you can prick the skins easily with a fork or a straw they are done. Take them out and put then on a dish. Keep the water. Next cut the oranges in half, pull out the pulp with a spoon, take out the pips and put them in a separate basin. Slice the orange peel very thinly (some people like it thick). Put the pulp back into the water, with the sugar, and boil. Then add the rinds and boil till it is done. Put a little on a plate, and if it thickens and sets when cool it is done.

Tie the pips in a piece of muslin, put them in a saucepan with a little water, boil them for a few minutes, then squeeze them and add the water to the marmalade. This gives the marmalade a slightly bitter taste.

PAW-PAW JAM.

1 large paw-paw, just turning yellow.
1 breakfast cup of water.
1 handful of native ginger (stem).
2 breakfast cups of sugar.

Peel the paw-paw, take away all the seeds, and cut up into small pieces. Put the water in the saucepan, add the pieces of paw-paw, the sugar and ginger. Boil for about 2 hours.

Don'ts—Do not let the saucepan burn; stir well before it starts to boil, then pull it back a little way and keep an eye on it, stirring occasionally till it is done.

HOME-MADE TOFFEE—1

4 tablespoons of butter.
1 breakfast cup of golden syrup.

2 breakfast cups of brown sugar.
A squeeze of lemon juice.

Melt the butter in a clean saucepan, then add the syrup, sugar and lemon juice, and one teaspoon of cold water. Let the sugar melt, then boil it steadily, keeping it well stirred all the time. When you think it is done drop a little into a cup of cold water. In a few seconds take out the piece, and if it snaps off crisply it is done; if not it requires more boiling. Pour it into buttered tins or plates, and leave it till it is cold. Before it quite sets it is a good thing to cut it across and across in little squares with a knife. It is then easier to break up when quite cold.

HOME-MADE TOFFEE—2.

1 breakfastcup of brown (Demerara) sugar.
3 tablespoons of butter.
2 tablespoons of milk.
1 teacup of golden syrup.

Melt the butter in a good, but old saucepan; add the sugar, milk and syrup. Boil slowly for 30 minutes, stirring the whole time. Pour into a greased tin and, before it sets too hard, mark and cut into squares. Nuts may be sprinkled on the toffee while it is hot. This is a very good toffee.

PEPPERMINT CREAMS.

1½ breakfast cups of icing sugar.
The white of an egg.
1 small tablespoon of cold water.
A few drops of essence of peppermint.

Sift the icing sugar. Add to it the white of a small egg and the water, and a few drops of peppermint. Mix these all together to a very firm paste, turn out on to a board and knead it with a little dry sugar.

Then roll it out and cut into rounds with a small cutter about the size of a penny. Dry them on grease-proof paper for 24 hours.

LEMON CURD.

2 tablespoons of butter.
2 whites of egg.
3 yolks.
1 breakfastcup of castor sugar.
2 lemons.

Melt the butter in an enamel pan; whisk the whites of egg and sugar well, and add them to it. Grate the rind of lemon, and strain the juice and add them. Stand the pan inside another one of boiling water. Stir the mixture well and boil till the mixture is thick. It can then be put in a jar and covered down till required.

TO BLANCH ALMONDS.

Have ready a saucepan of boiling water on the stove. Put the almonds into this for half-a-minute. Strain them and throw them at once into cold water. Skin them and dry them on a cloth.

OATMEAL PORRIDGE.

Remarks—The "medium" oatmeal is the best to use for this. The recipe below is enough for two men. This is the Scotch way of making porridge.

2 breakfast cups of water.
¾ teacup of oatmeal.
½ teaspoon of salt.

Put the water in a saucepan on the fire, and when it is just going to boil sprinkle in the meal with the left hand while you stir with the other, using a wooden spoon. This way prevents lumps. Keep stirring till it begins to boil. Boil for 10 minutes, then sprinkle in the salt and stir well. Boil for another 10 minutes, or longer, and it should then be ready to serve if it has been "jumping" all this time. But an hour is not too long to boil it. If cooked in this way it should never turn out a slimy mess, most indigestible and unpalatable.

Quaker Oats are easier to cook, and so I think better for this country as they do not require the same care or length of time while cooking as oatmeal porridge does if it is to be eatable. Make just in the same way as for oatmeal porridge.

HINTS FOR THE COOK'S BOX

It has been found by experience that it is better not to buy a "fitted" cook's box, but to get a strong wooden box and pack it with cooking utensils to one's own requirements, and fit it with a good padlock and key. The following are, I think, necessary.

1 iron kettle (oval), about 8 pints
1 small blocked tin kettle, about 3 pints
1 frying pan, about 6½ inches at bottom
A nest of aluminium saucepans:—

Diameter	Capacity
4½ inches	1 pint, good for sauces
6 inches	3 pints, (makes good cake tin)
8 inches	8½ pints, for soups, etc.
10 inches	15½ pints, for stews, etc.

Handles are extra, two would be sufficient—
6 inches
10 inches

These saucepans are expensive, but well worth the money. If, however, the iron ones are thought quite good enough they work out more cheaply:—
2 pints
4 pints
6 pints
10 pints

1 Cook's knife, 7 inches

1 wooden spoon, 10 inches
1 ordinary knife, spoon and fork
1 tin opener (strong)
1 corkscrew, all steel

2 pudding basins, white enamel— diam: 5½ inches; 7 inches
1 mixing bowl, white earthenware, 9½ inches
2 pie dishes, white enamel—9 inches; 11 inches
1 baking or oven tin, about 13 inches
Meat chopper

2 basins, enamel or tin, for washing up, 16 or 20 inches. These can be bought locally.
3 kitchen cloths about 1s. each
1½ yds. unbleached calico makes 2 pudding cloths—a good size is 22 inches x 19 inches.

The following may be added if desired :—

1 mincing machine "The Universal" is the simplest to clean
1 cheese grater and suet shredder combined
1 hair sieve, diameter: 9 inches

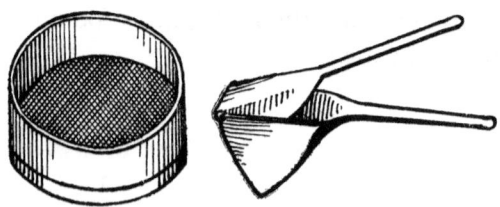

1 potato presser
1 pastry board, 18 inches x 14 inches
1 rolling pin
1 tin fish kettle about 18 inches, useful for boiling hams, etc.
1 large-size frying pan, 9½ inches at the bottom
1 1lb. bread tin
1 ½lb. cake tin or 6 inches across

1 toasting fork with wooden handle
1 scrubbing brush, a good one lasts longest
A set of pastry cutters, with plain or scalloped edge
2 inexpensive china jugs, about 1½ or 2 pints
2 ½-pint molds for jellies, these are best made of china
1 egg whisk, wire, 10 inches long

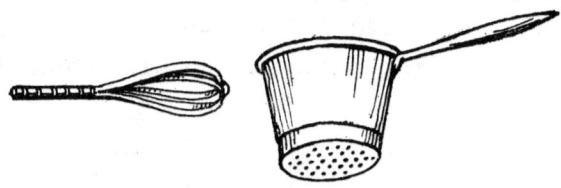

1 strainer enamel, for gravies, etc.
1 tin colander

Patty pans for tartlets and little cakes

A FEW SUBSTITUTES.

A glass bottle will serve for a rolling pin. The lid of a tin makes an emergency pastry cutter. If holes are pierced with a nail through the lid of a small tin it serves for a flour dredger, or sugar sifter. Holes pierced through the bottom of a tin (small holes) make an emergency gravy strainer. An aluminium saucepan, 6-inch size, does duty for a cake tin. A strip of wood off the lid of a wooden packing case makes a good knife board. The rim of a glass tumbler makes a good pastry cutter. An old clean kerosene tin makes an excellent boiler for a ham.

Bibliography

Boyle, Laura, 1968. *Diary of a Colonial Officer's Wife* (Oxford: Alden Press).

Chief Secretary's Office, Lagos, 1936. *The Nigeria Handbook* (London: West Africa Publicity Ltd.).

Kelly's Directories Ltd, 1940. *Kelly's Handbook to the Titled, Landed and Official Classes, 1940.* (London, Kelly's Directories Ltd).

Acknowledgements

This book is reprinted by kind permission of Muriel Tew's son, David Henderson Tew.

The editor acknowledges with sincere thanks the assistance of Jonathan Pike and Alex Hall.

Also available from Jeppestown Press:

Where the Lion Roars: An 1890 African Colonial Cookbook
Mrs A. R. Barnes

A reprint of one of Africa's earliest English-language cookery books, dating from 1890. Mrs Barnes' recipes for translucent, aromatic melon and ginger konfyt; fiery curries; and sweet peach chutney are as delicious now as they were a century ago; while instructions for making a canvas water cooler, and for treating venomous snake-bite or fever, offer a fascinating insight into the domestic lives of southern Africa's Victorian colonists. ISBN: 0-9553936-1-2

For full details of our inventory, or to order direct, view our web site at www.jeppestown.com

JEPPESTOWN

The Bulawayo Cookery Book and Household Guide
Edited by Mrs N. Chataway

This reprint of Zimbabwe's earliest cookery book is packed with recipes for Edwardian African delicacies: garnet-coloured tomato jam; fiery, home-made ginger beer and spicy bobotie. Packed with contemporary advertisements for companies like Puzey and Payne, Philpott and Collins and Haddon and Sly, the book even contains a section on veld cookery, contributed by Colonel Robert 'Boomerang' Gordon, D.S.O., O.B.E., who went on to raise and command the Northern Rhodesia Rifles at the outbreak of the First World War. ISBN: 0-9553936-2-0

For full details of our inventory, or to order direct, view our web site at www.jeppestown.com

JEPPESTOWN

The Anglo-African Who's Who 1907
Walter H. Wills (ed.)

A reprint of Walter Wills' quirky colonial reference book, containing the details of nearly 2,000 prominent men and women of Edwardian Africa. This astonishing work includes biographies of settlers, soldiers, explorers, politicians and traditional leaders from every corner of the continent. Invaluable for genealogists, historians, military researchers and medal enthusiasts, it offers details of over 1,200 separate medal awards, together with fascinating biographical sketches of colonial African celebrities—many of whom were known personally to the editor. ISBN: 0-9553936-3-9

For full details of our inventory, or to order direct, view our web site at www.jeppestown.com

JEPPESTOWN

The Rhodesia Medal Roll
David Saffery (ed)

Containing the names of nearly 13,000 recipients and revealing 2,300 previously unpublished decorations, this definitive book is the ultimate compendium of Rhodesian military and civilian honours and awards gazetted between 1970 and 1981. Fully indexed by surname, it is perfect for medal collectors and dealers, historians and genealogists—and a brilliant heirloom souvenir for recipients and their families. ISBN: 0-9553936-0-4

For full details of our inventory, or to order direct, view our web site at www.jeppestown.com

JEPPESTOWN

Matabeleland and the Victoria Falls
C. G. Oates (ed)

This book draws on the original diaries, letters, paintings and sketches of Frank Oates to paint a vivid picture of the Victorian exploration of Central Africa. It documents his encounters with legendary rulers such as King Lobengula of the Ndebele and larger-than-life characters like the ivory hunter Frederick Selous, and records Oates' final, fatal trek through the Zambezi Valley towards Victoria Falls. ISBN: 0955393647. ISBN-13: 978-0955393648

For full details of our inventory, or to order direct, view our web site at www.jeppestown.com

With Captain Stairs to Katanga
Joseph A. Moloney

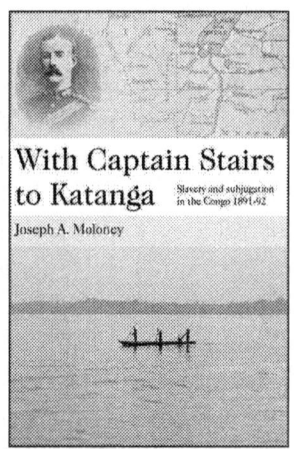

While British and Belgian companies greedily eyed the mineral riches of central Africa, a group of Victorian mercenaries marched nearly 1,000 miles through the bush to confront Msiri, the most powerful ruler in Katanga, and annex his kingdom. First published in 1893, this fascinating narrative will transport you to a world of cannibals, missionaries and slave traders; of a provocative military invasion and its bloody climax; and of the mercenaries' nightmarish return march—wracked by starvation and fever—back to the coast of East Africa. Containing a lively and detailed first-hand account of the 'scramble for Africa', this book is essential reading for anyone curious about the motivation and processes of European conquest in Africa. ISBN: 0-9553936-5-5

For full details of our inventory, or to order direct, view our web site at www.jeppestown.com

JEPPESTOWN

The Ghana Cookery Book
Various contributors

One of West Africa's earliest recipe books, the Ghana Cookery Book was first published in Accra in 1933. Over 800 recipes of recipes and contributors) make use of a wealth of local ingredients: ripe, tropical fruit, abundant fresh fish from the Atlantic Ocean, exotic spices, and a profusion of vegetables, grains and nuts from the fertile plantations of the Gold Coast. Providing a fascinating, unique snapshot of West African cuisine during the colonial period, the Ghana Cookery Book features a number of charming period advertisements, and is packed with vintage hints and tips on running a household in tropical Africa. If you have an interest in West Africa and the cultural histories of the region, this book makes for essential and enjoyable reading. ISBN: 0-9553936-6-3

For full details of our inventory, or to order direct, view our web site at www.jeppestown.com

JEPPESTOWN

10% discount! ORDER FORM

Use this form to order any of our books by post to addresses in the United Kingdom. For overseas orders please use the web site www.jeppestown.com.

Title	Price	Quantity	Total
Where the Lion Roars: An 1890 African Colonial Cookbook	~~£12.95~~ £11.66		
The Bulawayo Cookery Book and Household Guide	~~£12.95~~ £11.66		
The Anglo-African Who's Who 1907	~~£18.95~~ £17.06		
With Captain Stairs to Katanga	~~£12.95~~ £11.66		
The Ghana Cookery Book	~~£12.95~~ £11.66		
The Rhodesia Medal Roll	~~£17.95~~ £16.16		
Matabeleland and the Victoria Falls	~~£12.95~~ £11.66		
Cooking in West Africa	~~£12.95~~ £11.66		
Postage and packing within the UK			add £2.80
Total			

To order, send a cheque or postal order for the total amount (made payable to Jeppestown Press) to Jeppestown Press, 10A Scawfell St, London, E2 8NG.

Delivery details:
Name:
Address:

Telephone number (in case of query):

www.ingramcontent.com/pod-product-compliance
Lightning Source LLC
Chambersburg PA
CBHW071428160426
43195CB00013B/1845